THE FORBIDDEN CITY

紫禁城

五洲传播出版社
China Intercontinental Press

中华人民共和国万岁

前言

紫禁城（今故宫博物院），坐落于北京市中心，始建于明永乐四年（1406年），历时14年完成，为明（1368～1644年）、清（1644～1911年）两代帝王处理朝政和居住的皇宫，先后有24位皇帝（其中明朝14帝，清朝10帝）在此统治中国近500年。这座宫城规模宏大、气势磅礴，是世界上现存规模最大、最完整的古代木结构建筑群。

紫禁城占地面积为72万平方米，建筑面积15万平方米。紫禁城虽经明、清两代帝王多次重修和增建，但其建筑基本保持着初建时布局。宫城周围环绕10米多高的城墙，墙外是52米宽的护城河；宫墙四隅还建有四座精巧玲珑的角楼，构成一道严密的防御体系。城墙的四面各有一座城门，南面为午门，北面为神武门，东面为东华门，西面为西华门。

紫禁城名称的由来既包含着封建社会“天人合一”的思想，又与中国古代哲学和天文学有关。古代天文学把恒星分为三垣、二十八星宿，其中紫微星垣（北极星）居于正中，位置永恒不变，是所有星宿的中心。因此人们把紫微星视为天帝的居所，称为“紫宫”。封建皇帝自称是真龙天子，而他们所居住的皇宫，也被比喻为“紫宫”，象征四方归顺、江山稳固不变。皇帝贵为“九五之尊”，皇宫对于平民百姓来说，是绝对的禁地，无法涉足半步，所以，皇宫又被称为“禁宫”。除此之外，皇宫戒备森严，防御体系严密，是一座名副其实的“城中之城”。因此明清两代的皇宫被称为“紫禁城”。

紫禁城平面呈长方形，中轴布局，左右对称，主体建筑依次坐落在纵贯南北的中轴线上，其他建筑沿中轴线对称分布。紫禁城内部格局分为外朝和内廷。外朝的主体建筑为三大殿，即太和殿、中和殿和保和殿，又称“前三殿”，左右附有文华殿和武英殿，是皇帝举行大典、召见群臣和行使权力的地方。三大殿是皇权和威严的象征，因此居于宫城的中心位置，占地最广，殿顶或为重檐庑殿式，或为重檐歇山式，都与中国古代宫殿建筑规制相合。三座大殿坐落在8米多高的宽大台基之上，周围绕以石雕栏杆，栏杆望柱浮雕云龙、云凤图案。内廷以乾清宫、交泰殿、坤宁宫（统称后三宫）为中心，是皇帝处理政务以及皇室成员居住、游玩、奉神之处。内廷建筑布局严谨而富有生活气息。后三宫两侧分列出东西六宫，在明代是嫔妃们的居所，清代时后妃都可居住。西六宫的南面为养心殿，位居内廷而临近外朝。位于外东路的宁寿宫区在内廷中占地面积最大，是专供乾隆晚年归政居住的太上皇宫。宫城中轴线的尽端是御花园，体现了封建宫城规划“前宫后苑”的布局。园中有亭榭馆阁、殿堂，其间点缀着苍松翠柏、奇花异木、水池叠石等。

故宫博物院珍藏的文物近百万件，包括三代鼎彝、远古玉器、唐宋元明的书法名画、宋元陶瓷、珐琅、漆器、金银器、竹木牙角匏、金铜宗教造像以及大量的明清宫廷历史文物，如帝后妃嫔服饰、衣料和家具等。此外，还有大量图书典籍、文献档案。1961年，故宫博物院被列为全国重点文物保护单位。1987年，联合国教科文组织将故宫列为“世界文化遗产”。现在，故宫除了保存和复原三大殿、后三宫和西六宫等处的原状陈列之外，还设有青铜器、陶瓷、工艺、书画、钟表、珍宝等专馆。这座古老而又宏伟的皇家宫殿，向广大中外游客展现出了中华民族悠久深远的历史和灿烂辉煌的文化，被誉为“世界五大宫殿之一”。

PREFACE 【英文】

Located in the heart of Beijing, the Forbidden City (known as the Palace Museum today) was built in the fourth year of Emperor Yongle's reign (1406), and completed 14 years later. The Forbidden City, used as the Imperial Palace in the Ming (1368-1644) and Qing (1644-1911) dynasties, housed 24 emperors (14 of the Ming and 10 of the Qing) for as long as 500 years. This grand and majestic complex is the largest and completed wooden cluster in the world today.

The Forbidden City covers a total area of 720,000 square meters, with the building area of 150,000 square meters. Though repaired and extended in the Ming and Qing dynasties, the Forbidden City remains its original layout. The palace was surrounded by the 10-meter-high walls, outside which runs the 52-meter-wide moat, and on each corner sits a corner tower, composing a strong defense work. There open four gates, namely, Meridian Gate in the south, Gate of Martial Spirit in the north, East Flowery Gate in the east and West Flowery Gate in the west.

The name of the Forbidden City is related to the concept of "Human and Nature in One" in China's feudal society and China's ancient philosophy and astronomy, according to which, there were three enclosures and 28 stars in the universe, of which the Purple Forbidden Enclosure (Polaris), thought to be in the middle of all stars, was seen to be where heavenly emperor lived and was called Purple Palace. The emperor regarded himself as the son of Heaven, and the Imperial Palace was called Purple Palace, symbolizing that all is submitted to the emperor and the rule over the country is steady and unchangeable. The Imperial Palace where the honored emperor lived had tight security, and the access of ordinary people was completely forbidden. Besides, the imperial palace, with heavily-guarded and strict defensive works, seems as a real city in the city. Thus the Imperial Palace during the Ming and Qing dynasties was called the Purple Forbidden City.

In the rectangular palace city, main structures stand on the central axis one by one and other architectural structures are laid out symmetrically along the central axis. The Outer Court and Inner Court consist of the inner layout of the palace city. The Outer Court is centered on Three Grand Halls or Three Front Halls, namely, Hall of Supreme Harmony, Hall of Middle Harmony and Hall of Preserving Harmony, which are flanked by Hall of Literary Glory and Hall of Martial Valor. The Outer Court is where the emperor held grand ceremonies, summoned ministers and wielded power. The Three Grand Halls, demonstrating the supremacy of imperial power, lie in the center of the palace city and covers a vast area, with double-eaved hip or saddle roofs, which are coincidence with the Chinese ancient classification of construction. The Three Grand Halls are situated on an eight-meter-high white-marble base surrounded by stone balustrades designed with the patterns of dragon and phoenix in the cloud. The Inner Court, centered on the Palace of Heavenly Purity, Hall of Union and Peace and Palace of Earthly Tranquility, jointedly called Three Back Palaces, was the residential area where the emperor handled state affairs and the royal family members lived, amused and worshipped the Gods. The Six Eastern Palaces and Six Western Palaces on both sides of the Three Back Palaces were the residences

for the Ming concubines and the Qing empresses and concubines. To the south of the Six Western Palaces is the Hall of Mental Cultivation, which is close to the Outer Court. Palace of Tranquility and Longevity, lying in the outer east and covering the largest area in the Inner Court, was initially built for Emperor Qianlong to live after his abdication. At the end of the central axis of the Forbidden City is the Imperial Garden, fully showing the layout of the feudal imperial palaces - palaces in the front and gardens in the rear. Halls and pavilions are laid out orderly, dotted with green pines, cypresses, rare flowers, stones and ponds, etc.

Around one million pieces of relics are collected in the Palace Museum, including Ding (the ancient cooking vessel), Yi (the ancient wine vessel), jades, calligraphy and paintings of Tang, Song, Yuan and Ming dynasties, china wares of Song and Yuan dynasties, enamel wares, lacquer wares, gold and silver items, bamboo and ivory carvings, religious statues, as well as imperial relics like attires and furniture used by emperors, empresses and concubines. Additionally, there were a lot of books, classics, and document files. In 1961, the Forbidden City became one of the key units for preservation of cultural relics.

In 1987, the Forbidden City was inscribed into the World Heritage List by the UNESCO. At present, there is not only the display of the original states of palaces like Three Grand Halls, Three Back Palaces and Six Western Palaces, but also the specific exhibition halls for various kinds of historical and cultural relics. This ancient and magnificent architectural complex, famed as one of the Five Palaces in the world, displays its historical and cultural beauty to all visitors home and abroad.

INTRODUCTIONE 【法文】

Située au centre de Beijing, la Cité pourpre interdite (le musée du Palais impérial d'aujourd'hui) fut construite à partir de 1406, à savoir dans la 4e année du règne de l'empereur Yongle sous la dynastie des Ming, et réalisée pendant 14 ans. Dans ce Palais impérial, où les empereurs des dyanasties des Ming et des Qing traitèrent les affaires politiques et résidèrent, 24 empereurs (14 des Ming et 10 des Qing) gouvernèrent la Chine pendant 500 ans. Grandiose et majestueuse, cette Cité représente l'ancien complexe architectural de bois le plus vaste et le mieux conservé, existant de nos jours au monde.

La Cité interdite couvre 720 000 m² dont 150 000 m² de constructions. En ayant connu plusieurs reprises sous les Ming et les Qing, la Cité interdite maintient son architecture initiale. Entourée par une muraille de 10 mètres de haut, elle-même cernée d'une douve large de 52 mètres, la Cité interdite abrite quatre tours finement travaillées dans les quatre angles, et quatre portes dans les quatre côtés : Porte du Midi au sud, Porte de la Prouesse divine au nord, Porte de la Gloire orientale à l'est, Porte de la Gloire occidentale à l'ouest, tout ce qui constitue un système rigoureux de défense.

La dénomination de la Cité pourpre interdite englobe l'idée de « l'unité entre le Ciel et l'Homme », mais se rapporte également à la philosophie et l'astronomie anciennes de Chine. Dans l'astronomie ancienne, les étoiles sont divisées en 28 constellations et trois étoiles, dont la petite étoile violette (l'étoile polaire) est perpétuellement au centre de toutes les constellations. La petite étoile violette est donc considérée comme la résidence de l'Empereur Céleste, appelée « Palais violet ». Les empereurs dans la société féodale ancienne se disaient « fils du ciel » et leur résidence fut également « palais violet », qui symbolise le ralliement de tous les coins du pays et le pouvoir stable. L'accès au Palais impérail était absolument interdit au peuple. Le Palais impérial fut donc appelé « palais interdit ». Par ailleurs, étant sur le qui-vive, le Palais impérial possède un système de défense rigoureux et est une véritable « cité dans la cité ». C'est ainsi que le Palais impérial sous les dynasties des Ming et des Qing est appelé « Cité pourpre interdite ».

Sur un plan rectangulaire, la Cité interdite est symétrique sur un axe central sud-nord, sur lequel se situent les principales constructions. D'autres se répartissent de façon symétrique le long de l'axe sud-nord. La Cité interdite est divisée en deux parties : la Cour extérieure et la Cour intérieure. La Cour extérieure abrite principalement trois salles : la salle de l'Harmonie Suprême, la salle de l'Harmonie Parfaite et la salle de l'Harmonie Préservée, appelées aussi « salles antérieures », qui sont accompagnés des bâtiments latéraux dont la salle de la Gloire Littéraire et la salle des Prouesses Militaires. C'était là où l'empereur présidait des grandes cérémonies officielles, recevait ses ministres et exerçait son pouvoir. Les trois salles, symbols de l'autorité et la dignité impériales, se trouvent au centre de la Cour extérieure et occupent une place plus grande. Leur toiture, soit aux avant-toits doublés avec cinq faîtes, soit aux avant-toits avec neuf faîtes, correspond aux règles architecturales des palais anciens de la Chine. Ces trois salles se trouvent toutes sur une immense terrasse ceinturée de balustrades et de colonnes sculptées de dragons, de phénix et de nuages. La Cour intérieure, centrée sur les trois palais postérieurs qui sont le palais de la Pureté Céleste, la salle de l'Union et le palais de la Tranquilité terrestre, était l'endroit où l'empereur traitait les affaires politiques, les membres de la famille impériale habitaient, jouaient et offraient des sacrifices aux dieux. L'architecture de la Cour intérieure est rigoureuse mais riche en saveurs de la vie. Les trois palais postérieurs sont flanqués des « six palais de l'Est » et des « six palais de l'Ouest », qui servaient d'habitations des concubines des dynasties des Ming et des Qing. Au sud des « six palais de l'Ouest » se trouve le palais de la Nourriture de l'Esprit, qui relève de la Cour intérieure, mais proche de la Cour extérieure. Le palais de la Tranquilité et de la Longévité dans l'est de la Cour intérieure, qui occupe une place plus grande que les autres palais et salles, était destiné à l'habitation de Qianlong après son abdication. Le Jardin impérial se trouve à l'extrémité de l'axe central, ce qui présente une disposition de la cité impériale dans la société féodale, marquée par « palais en avant et jardin en arrière ». Le Jardin impérial abrite des kiosques, pavillions, salles, qui sont embellis de pins, de sapin, de fleurs et arbres rares, d'étangs et de pierres superposées.

Le musée du Palais impérial collectionne 1 million d'objets culturels, parmi lesquels des trépieds, des objets de jade remontant à la haute antiquité, des oeuvres picturales et calligraphiques datant des dynasties des Tang, des Song, des Yuan et des Ming, des céramiques des Song et des Yuan, des émaux, des objets de laque, d'or et d'argent, des sculptures en bambau, bois, ivoire ou corne, des statues religieuses d'or et de bronze, ainsi qu'un grand nombre d'objets datant des Ming et des Qing, dont vêtements et parures portés par les empereurs, les impératrices et les concubines, des tissus et meubles. On y trouve encore une quantité de livres et textes anciens, de documents et dossiers. En 1961, le musée du Palais impérial a été classé parmi les monuments historiques placés sous la protection de l'Etat. En 1987, il a été inscrit à la liste du patrimoine mondial culturel par l'UNESCO. Maintenant, le Palais impérial rétablit et conserve l'ameublement originaire des trois salles antérieures, des trois palais postérieurs ainsi que des « six palais de l'Ouest ». Au-delà de cela, des salles spéciales sont destinées à l'exposition des bronzes, céramiques, objets de l'artisanat, oeuvres picturales et calligraphiques, horloges et montres, de la bijouterie, etc. Ce Palais impérial, ancien et majestueux, montre la longue histoire et la civilisation brillante de la nation chinoise, classé parmi les « cinq palais du monde ».

VORWORT 【德文】

Die Purpurne Verbotene Stadt (heute Palastmuseum), auch der Kaiserpalast genannt, liegt im Zentrum der Stadt Beijing. Ihre Bauarbeiten begannen im 4. Jahr (1406) der Yongle-Regierungsperiode der Ming-Dynastie und dauerten 14 Jahre. Sie diente als Residenz der Ming- und Qing-Dynastie. Von hier aus regierten insgesamt 24 Kaiser (14 Ming-Kaiser und 10 Qing-Kaiser) etwa 500 Jahre lang das ganze Land. Die Purpurne Verbotene Stadt ist der größte und vollständigste Baukomplex in Holzkonstruktion der Welt .

Die Purpurne Verbotene Stadt nimmt eine Gesamtfläche von 720 000 Quadratmetern ein und ihre Baufläche beträgt 150 000 Quadratmeter. Obwohl sie seit ihrer Entstehung mehrmals umgebaut wurde, bleibt sie bis heute unverändert. Rings um die Purpurnen Verbotenen Stadt sieht man eine über 10 m hohe Stadtmauer und außerhalb der Stadtmauer einen 52 m breiten Wallgraben. An jeder der vier Mauerecken gibt es einen eigenartigen Wachtturm und an jeder der vier Seiten der Stadtmauer ein Stadttor: das Wumen-Tor im Süden, das Shenwumen-Tor im Norden, das Donghuamen-Tor im Osten und das Xihuamen-Tor im Westen.

Der Name der Purpurnen Verbotenen Stadt kommt aus dem Gedanken der „Harmonie zwischen Natur und Menschen" der feudalen Gesellschaft und hat mit der antiken chinesischen Astronomie zu tun. Der Große Bär, früher auf Chinesisch Ziwei-Stern genannt, diente als Wohnstätte mit dem Namen „Zigong" (Purpurne Stadt) für den Himmelskaiser. Der Kaiser wurde als Himmelssohn betrachtet. So wurde seine Wohnstätte auch als „Purpurne Stadt" bezeichnet und symbolisierte die Stabiltät seiner Herrschaft. Darüber hinaus war seine Wohnstätte für das einfache Volk eine verbotene Zone. Das war der Grund, warum der Kaiserpalast der Ming- und Qing-Dynastie als die Purpurne Verbotene Stadt bezeichnet wurde.

Die Purpurne Verbotene Stadt zeichnet sich durch ihre imposante Ausstattung, ihre strenge Planung und die integrierte und symmetrische Anordnung des gesamten Baukomplexes aus. Ihre wichtigen Bauten befinden sich auf einer in süd-nördlicher Richtung führenden Zentralachse und die anderen Bauten liegen symmetrisch an ihren beiden Seiten. Die Purpurne Verbotene Stadt ist in drei Teile – den Außenhof, den Innenhof und den Palastgarten – gegliedert. Der Außenhof mit den drei Haupthallen Taihedian (Halle der Höchsten Harmonie), Zhonghedian (Halle der Vollkommenen Harmonie) und Baohedian (Halle der Erhaltung der Harmonie) mit Mittelpunkt liegt im Süden. Hier empfing der Kaiser hohe Beamte, übte seine Macht aus und hielt wichtige Zeremonien ab. An der linken und rechten Seite dieser drei Haupthallen liegen die Wenhuadian (Halle der Literarischen Blüte) und die Wuyingdian (Halle der Militärischen Tapferkeit). Die drei Haupthallen liegen auf einem 8 m hohen Postament, das von Marmorbalustraden umgeschlossen ist. Hinter dem Außenhof liegt der Innenhof, wo der Kaiser mit seinen Familienangehörigen lebte und laufende Staatsangelegenheiten erledigte. Der Innenhof besteht aus den drei Hauptpalästen Qianqinggong (Palast der Himmlischen Reinheit), Jiaotaidian (Halle der Berührung von Himmel und Erde) und Kunninggong (Palast der Irdischen Ruhe), den sechs östlichen und den sechs westlichen Palästen, der Yangxindian (Halle zur Bildung der Gefühle) und dem Ningshou-Palast. Die sechs östlichen und die sechs westlichen Paläste waren in der Ming-Zeit als Schlafgemächer für die Konkubinen des Kaisers bestimmt. In der Qing-Zeit wohnten die Konkubinen der gestorbenen Kaiser ebenfalls hier. Der Ningshou-Palast ist der größte Palast im Innenhof. Der Qing-Kaiser Qian Long lebte hier, nachdem er dem Thron entsagte hatte. Der Palastgarten liegt im Norden des Innenhofes. Er ist nicht allzu groß, aber schön und ideal plaziert, mit uralten Kiefern und Zypressen, Blumen und Bambus, künstlichen Felsanlagen und Springbrunnen, Lauben und Pavillons.

Die Purpurne Verbotene Stadt ist eine große Schatzkammer. Hier werden eine Million kostbare Kulturgegenstände aus verschiedenen Dynastien gesammelt, darunter Ding (antike Kochgefäße mit zwei Handgriffen und drei oder vier Beinen), Jadewaren, malerische und kalligrafische Werke aus den Dynastien Tang, Song, Yuan und Ming, Porzellan-, Lack-, Email-, Gold- und Silberwaren, Gold- und Bronzebuddhafiguren aus den Dynastien Song und Yuan sowie Kleider und Möbel aus den Dynastien Ming und Qing. Darüber hinaus werden hier auch große Mengen von Büchern und Dokumenten aufbewahrt.

Im Jahre 1961 wurde die Purpurne Verbotene Stadt zum Schwerpunkt des Denkmalschutzes erklärt. Im Jahre 1987 wurde sie von der UNESCO in die Liste des Weltkulturerbes aufgenommen. Heute sind die drei Haupthallen im Außenhof, die drei Hauptpaläste und die sechs westlichen Paläste im Innenhof wurden originalgetreu renoviert. Die sechs östlichen Paläste sowie die Fengxian-Halle und der Fastenpalast dienen heute als Ausstellungshallen über Bronzewaren, Porzellanwaren, kunsthandwerkliche Produkte, Malerei und Kalligrafie, Uhren und Kostbarkeiten. Heute ist die Purpurne Verbotene Stadt als einer der fünf größten Paläste der Welt bekannt.

Предисловие 【俄文】

Запретный город находится в самом центре Пекина. Строительство его началось в 1406 г. и продолжалось на 14 г. Это дворцовый ансамбль, служивший резиденцией для 24 императоров династий Мин и Цин (среди них 14 минских императоров и 10 цинских императоров), которые господствовали в Китае около 500 лет. По своим размерам Гугун является самым большим и целостным из сохранившихся древних дворцовых ансамблей в мире.

Общая площадь Запретного города – 720 тыс. кв. км, площадь сооружений – 150 тыс. кв. км. Дворцовый ансамбль окружен стеной высотой 10 м и рвом с водой шириной 52 м. В четырех углах стены возведены 4 угловые башни. Все это образовало крепкую систему обороны. На каждой из 4 сторон стены есть ворота. Ворота на южной стороне – Умэнь, ворота на северной – Шэньумэнь, на восточной – Дунхуамэнь, на западной – Сихуамэнь.

В древней астрономии звезды разделяются на 3 юань (юань является сравнительно широким районом, где есть много созвездий) и 28 синсю (созвездие). Цзывэйсин, один из трех юаней, находится в самом центре неба и является центром всех созвездий. Поэтому люди считали, что на Цзывэйсин проживает небесный царь, и назвали его Цзыгуном (пурпурный дворец). Феодальные императоры считали себя сыновьями дракона. Дворец, где они жили, были названы Цзыгуном. Плюс, запретили простого народа приблизиться к великолепному императорскому дворцу. Поэтому императорский дворец при династиях Мин и Цин называется Цзыцзинчэн (Пурпурный Запретный город).

План Запретного города – прямоугольный. Сооружения на севере к Умэнь разделяются на внешние павильоны и внутренние резиденции. Главными сооружениями внешних павильонов – павильоны Тайхэдянь, Чжунхэдянь и Баохэдянь. К тому же, на востоке и западе еще находятся павильоны Вэньхуадянь и Уиндянь, которые предназначались для проведения важнейших государственных и придворных церемониалов. Тайхэдянь, Чжунхэдянь и Баохэдянь – символ императорской власти, поэтому они находятся в центре Запретного города и занимают крупнейшую площадь в нем. Эти три павильона расположены на трех платформах высотой 8 м. Павильоны Цяньцингун, Цзяотайдянь и Куньнингун находятся в центре внутренних резиденций. Здесь император занимался государственными делами, а императрица, наложницы императора, принцы и принцессы жили, играли и приносили жертву богу. На обеих сторонах Цяньцингун, Цзяотайдянь и Куннингун стоят 12 павильонов, которые предназначены для проживания наложниц при династии Мин и для наложниц и императриц при династии Цин. К югу от 6 западных павильонов – павильон Янсиньдянь. И район Ниншоугун занимает самую большую площадь во внутренних резиденциях. Он служил резиденцией цинского императора Цяньлун, который в своей старости передал наследнику престол. В самом северном конце центральной оси – императорский сад, где есть не только беседки, терема, но и изумительные цветы и растения.

В Гугуне хранятся миллион ценных памятников. Среди них есть и нефритовые изделия глубокой древности, каллиграфии и известные картины династий Тан, Сун, Юань и Мин, сунская и юньская керамика, эмали, лаковые изделия, золотые и серебряные изделия, религиозные статуи из золота и меди, еще и многочисленные одежды цинских императриц, ткани, мебель и т.д. В 1961 г. музей Гугун был занесен в памятники культуры Китая. В 1987 г. он был занесен ЮНЕСКО в реестр объектов мирового культурного наследия.

Remparts et fossé Die Stadtmauer und der Wallgraben Стена и ров

CITY STRUCTURE

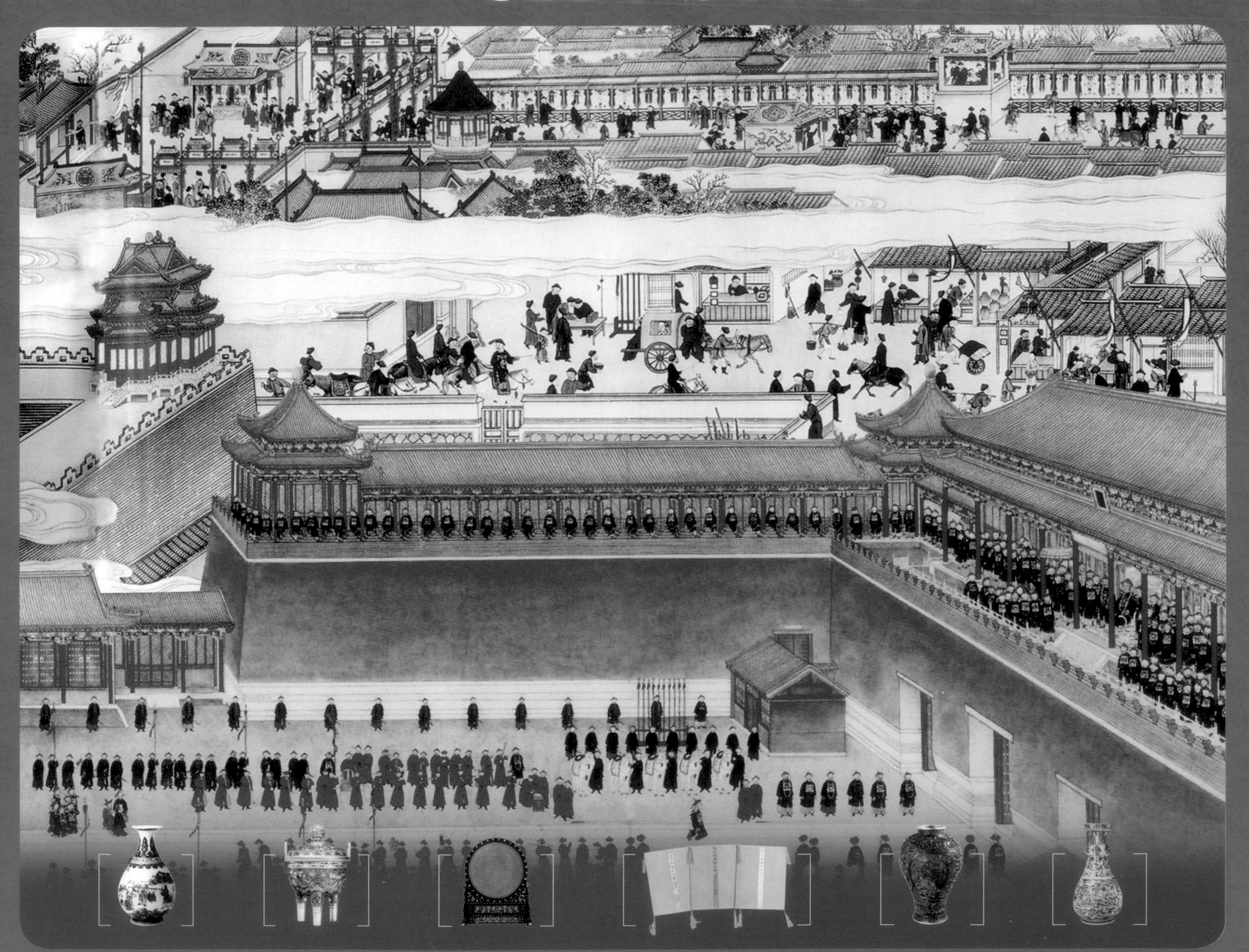

城池 CITY STRUCTURE

Remparts et fossé Die Stadtmauer und der Wallgraben Стена и ров

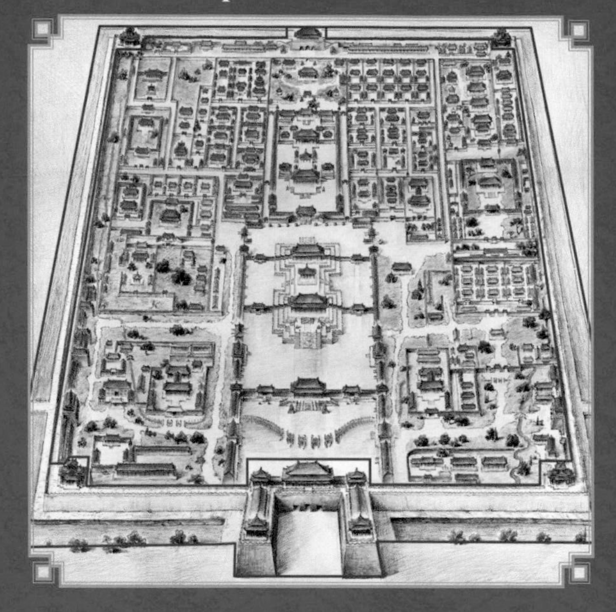

城池：紫禁城宫城四周建有高10米的城墙。墙外是52米宽、6米深的护城河，全用条石砌岸。城墙四隅各建一座精美的角楼，构成了一道牢固的防卫屏障。城墙四面各有一座城门，南为午门，北为神武门，东为东华门，西为西华门。

City Structure【英文】The Forbidden City is surrounded by a 10-meter-tall wall and a 52-meter-wide and six-meter-deep moat, whose bank was lined with bricks. On each corner of the wall stands a corner tower. All of these constitute the strong defensive barrier of the Forbidden City. Besides, there are four gates, namely, Meridian Gate in the south, Gate of Martial Spirit in the north, East Flowery Gate in the east and West Flowery Gate in the west.

Remparts et fossé【法文】La Cité interdite est entourée par une muraille de dix mètres de haut, elle-même contournée par une douve large de 52 mètres et profonde de 6, avec les rives bâties de plaques de pierres. Une tour finement travaillée se dresse à chaque angle de la muraille. Tout ceci constitue une barrière de défense solide. Dans les quatre côtés de la muraille se trouvent quatre portes : Porte du Midi au sud, Porte de la Prouesse divine au nord, Porte de la Gloire orientale à l'est, Porte de la Gloire occidentale à l'ouest.

Die Stadtmauer und der Wallgraben【德文】Rings um die Purpurne Verbotene Stadt sieht man eine 10 m hohe Stadtmauer. Außerhalb dieser Stadtmauer liegt ein 52 m breiter und 6 m tiefer Wallgraben, der aus rechteckigen Steinplatten angelegte wurde. An jeder der vier Mauerecken gibt es einen Wachtturm. Die Stadtmauer hat vier Stadttore: das östliche Tor heisst Wumen, das nördliche Tor Shenwumen, das östliche Tor Donghuamen und das westliche Tor Xihuamen.

Стена и ров【俄文】С четырех сторон Запретный город окружен стеной высотой 10 м. Вне стены – ров с водой шириной 52 м и глубиной 6 м. На каждой из четырех сторонах стены возведена своеобразная угловая башня. Все это образовало крепкую систему обороны. На четырех сторонах стены есть четыре пары ворот: Дунхуамэнь на востоке, Умэнь на юге, Сихуамэнь на западе и Шэньумэнь на севере.

城墙是城池的主体建筑。紫禁城四周建有高10米，长3.5千米的城墙。城墙平面呈梯形，上窄下宽，上宽6.66米，下宽8.62米。城墙外用青砖砌成，内用夯土填筑，是皇宫外围的一道坚固的防御设施。

City Wall【英文】As the main part of the city structure, the city wall stands 10 meters tall and extends 3.5 kilometers long. The trapezoidal wall is narrower at the top (6.66 meters wide) yet wider on the base (8.62 meters wide). The wall, built by bricks in the exterior and earth in the interior, composes the strong defense work of the outer Imperial Palace.

Muraille【法文】La muraille constitue la construction principale d'une ville ancienne. Les alentous de la Cité interdite sont entourés par une muraille de 10 mètres de haut et de 3,5 mètres de long. Le plan de la muraille est en forme de trapèze, large de 6,66 mètres en haut et 8,62 en bas. La muraille, bâtie avec des briques bleues et damée de sol à son intérieur, représente une défense solide à l'extérieur du Palais impérial.

Die Stadtmauer【德文】Die Stadtmauer ist 10 m hoch und 3,5 km lang, oben 6,66 m und unten 8,62 m breit. Sie besteht innen aus Erde und außen aus schwarzen Ziegelsteinen und stellt eine feste Schutzanlage außerhalb des Kaiserpalastes dar.

Стена【俄文】Вокруг Запретного города была построена стена высотой 10 м, длиной 3,5 км. Продольное сечение городской стены – трапециевидно. Наверху – узко, внизу – широко. Верхняя ширина – 6,66 м, нижняя ширина – 8,82 м. Эта стена является крепким оборонным объектом вне императорского дворца.

各色釉大瓶（清）
A Qing Dynasty glazed vase
Vase émaillé multicolore datant des Qing
Buntfarbig glasierte Vase (Qing-Dynastie)
Большая фарфоровая ваза, покрытая картинами (династия Цин)

画珐琅八宝纹法轮（清）
A Qing Dynasty painted enameled Dharma-wheel
Roue de la Loi en émail à dessins de huit trésors des Qing
Acht-Schätze-Rad, ein Kultgerät (Qing-Dynastie)
Колесо Дхармы эмалевое с восьми видами узоров (династия Цин)

护城河

护城河河面宽52米，深6米，环绕于城墙外围。明末李自成率领的农民起义军攻入紫禁城时，未被崇祯皇帝宠信的宫女投河自尽，以死效忠皇帝。自清康熙年间，护城河里栽种莲藕，除部分供应宫中膳食外，剩下的都拿到市场上去卖，所得收入用于宫中日常开销。护城河水的源头是京西的玉泉山，玉泉山水经过颐和园、西直门的高梁桥，流到市中心的后海，然后从地安门的布梁桥下分出支流，经景山西门的地道流进护城河。

The Moat【英文】 Outside the city wall runs the moat, which is 52 meters wide and six meters deep. At the end of the Ming Dynasty, when the peasant uprisings led by Li Zicheng forced into the Forbidden City, the unloved maids of Emperor Chongzhen (r. 1627-1644) made holes in the water to show their sincerity to this last Ming emperor. Since the reign of Emperor Kangxi (1661-1722) in the Qing Dynasty, lotus rhizomes were planted in the moat: some were used to supply the meals in the palace, and the rest were sold on the market, the earnings of which were used for daily expenses. The river of the moat springs from Jade Spring Mountain in the west suburbs of Beijing. And the water flows through the Summer Palace, Gaoliang Bridge in Xizhimen area, Back Lake in the downtown, and passes across the Buliang Bridge in Di'anmen area. Then one tributary stream flows into the moat through a tunnel underground the west gate of Jingshan Park.

Douve【法文】 La douve, large de 52 mètres et profonde de 6, contourne l'extérieur de la muraille. Lorsque l'armée des paysans dirigée par Li Zicheng attaquait la Cité interdite, les dames de cour qui n'avaient jamais gagné la faveur de l'empereur Chongzhen se sont suicidées en jetant dans la douve, afin de faire preuve de loyauté envers l'empereur. Depuis le règne de l'empereur Kangxi des Qing, les lotus étaient plantés dans la douve. Des racines de lotus étaient offertes à la cour impériale et le reste, vendu sur le marché. Les recettes de vente étaient destinées à la compensation des dépenses courantes de la cour.

Der Wallgraben【德文】 Der Wallgraben, auch Tongzi-Fluss genannt, liegt außerhalb der Stadtmauer des Kaiserpalastes. Er ist 52 m breit und 6 m tief. Ende der Ming-Dynastie stürzten sich viele Hofmädchen zum Selbstmord hier ins Wasser, bevor die Soldaten der aufständischen Bauernarmee mit Li Zicheng an der Spitze in die Purpurne Verbotene Stadt eindrangen. Seit der Regierungsperiode des Qing-Kaisers Kang Xi begann man Lotos in diesem Wallgraben anzubauen. So konnten Kaiser und seine Familienmitglider im Sommer nicht nur schöne Lotosblumen bewundern, sondern auch im Herbst und Winter die aus Lotoswurzeln zubereiteten Speisen genießen.

Ров с водой【俄文】 Вне городской стены есть широкий ров, наполненный водой. Ширина его – 52 м, глубина – 6 м. При правлении цинского императора Канси в этом рве началось выращивать лотос. Часть корневищей лотоса была представлена для кухонь в Запретном городе. А остальные были проданы на рынке. Доходы от них были употреблены для ежедневной траты города.

嵌宝“金瓯永固”金杯（清）
A Qing Dynasty gemmy gold cup
Weinbecher aus Gold (Qing-Dynastie
Coupe en or incrustée de perles des Qing
Золотой бокал, украшенный драгоценностями,
символизирующий вечность династии Цин (династия Цин)

画珐琅山水人物瓶（清）
A Qing Dynasty painted enameled vase
Vase en émail au paysage et aux portraits des Qing
Emailenvase mit Menschenfiguren (Qing-Dynastie)
Эмалевая ваза, покрытая картиной горы,
реки и человека (династия Цин)

角楼

紫禁城城墙上有四座角楼，造型精巧，结构独特，是中国古建的精品。屋顶为三重檐的方形楼亭，上覆黄琉璃瓦。角楼通过72条脊衔接，内没有柱子，外没有梁头。无论从哪个角度看，角楼呈现的都是正面。

Corner Tower【英文】 On each corner of the wall stands a corner tower, of fine workmanship and distinctive structures. As the exquisite works among the ancient buildings, the square corner towers are designed with three-tiered eaves and covered with yellow glazed tiles. They are connected by 72 ridges, with neither columns inside nor beams outside. From any angle, we always see the front side of the corner tower.

Tours d'angle【法文】 Les quatre tours d'angle sur la muraille de la Cité interdite, de forme ingénieuse et de structure originale, représentent des chef d'oeuvres de l'architecture ancienne chinoise. La toiture à triple avant-toit est couverte de tuiles jaunes vernissées. Jointe par 72 faîtes, la tour d'angle n'a ni colonne à son intérieur ni poutre à son extérieur. Sous n'importe quel angle, la tour présente la façade.

Ecktürme【德文】 Auf der Stadtmauer des Kaiserpalastes gibt es vier Ecktürme. Jeder von diesen quadratischen Wachttürmen hat ein dreifaches Dach aus gelb grasierten Ziegeln und besteht aus 9 Balken, 18 Stützsäulen und 72 Dachfirsten.

Угловая башня【俄文】 На четырех углах стены Запретного города стоят 4 угловые башни замысловатой формой, которые представляют собой шедевр древнего зодчества Китая. Крыша башни трехъярусная и покрыта желтыми глазурными черепицами. Конструкция башни уникальна. Независимо от того, с какой стороны посмотреть, всегда показан именно фасад башни.

犀角雕云龙杯（明）
A Ming Dynasty rhinoceros horn carved cup
Coupe en corne de rhinocéros sculptée de dessins de nuage et de dragon, datant des Ming
Weinbecher aus Horn des Nashorns (Qing-Dynastie)
Чаша с узорами облака и дракона из рога носорога (династия Мин)

午门

午门为紫禁城的正门，总高38米，是紫禁城最高的一座建筑，分为台基和楼体两部分。城台呈“凹”字形，台上建有五座重檐黄瓦的城楼，称为“五凤楼”。午门是国家重要的典仪举行的场所。例如，战争凯旋举行献俘仪式；每年孟冬颁发次年使用的历书；每年立春，京城县令将象征春耕的春牛、春山（一种装饰性的牌坊）由午门抬入宫中，进献给皇帝、太后和皇后等。

Meridian Gate【英文】The Meridian Gate, being the City's front gate, is the tallest building in the Forbidden City, with the maximum height of 38 meters. The base takes a “凹” shape, on which five skirt-roof towers covered with yellow glazed tiles are built. These five towers together are called Five Phoenix Tower. The Meridian Gate was ceremonial. Some major events such as the receiving of the captives of war, the ceremony of issuing the official lunar calendar were held here. On every spring begins, local officials in the capital city would enter into the Forbidden City through this gate to offer the clay cattle and decorative memorial archways, which represent spring ploughing, to the emperor, empress and empress dowager.

Porte du Midi【法文】La Porte du Midi, qui est l'entrée principale de la Cité interdite, d'une hauteur de 38 mètres, est la plus haute construction de la Cité interdite. Elle comprend eux parties : la terrasse de forme « U » et les tours. Les cinq tours surmontant la terrasse, à double avant-toit et de jaunes tuiles vernissées, sont appelées « Cinq Tours de Phénix ». Devant la Porte du Midi, étaient organisées des grandes cérémonies d'Etat. Par exemple : la remise des prisonniers de guerre après une triomphe, l'annonce du nouveau calendrier dans le premier mois de l'hiver. Dans la 1ère quinzaine de l'année qui commence vers le 4 février, des boeufs et des portiques décoratifs symbolisant le labourage printanier, offerts par les chefs de districts de la capitale à l'empereur, l'impératrice et l'impératrice douairière, étaient transportés au Palais impérial à travers la Porte du Midi.

Das Wumen-Tor【德文】Das Wumen-Tor, allgemein Wufenglou (Turm der Fünf Phönixe) genannt, ist der Haupteingang zum Kaiserpalast. Mit einer Höhe von 38 m ist es das höchste Bauwerk des Kaiserpalastes. Der Unterteil des Tors besteht aus einer 10 m hohen, zinnoberroten U-förmigen Mauer. Darauf stehen fünf Tortürme mit Doppeldächern aus gelb glasierten Ziegeln. Früher wurden hier wichtige Zeremonien abgehalten. Kamen Generäle zum Beispiel von einem triumphalen Feldzug zurück, fand hier eine Zeremonie zur Überreichung der Kriegsgefangenen statt. Alljährlich im 10. Mondmonat wurde hier der Kalender für das nächste Jahr erlassen. Und alljährlich am Tag des Frühlingsbeginns brachte der örtliche Kreisvorsteher Rinderfiguren aus Papier durch dieses Tor in den Kaiserhof, um sie als Symbol der Frühjahresbestellung dem Kaiser, seiner Mutter und Frau darzubieten.

Умэнь【俄文】Ворота Умэнь являются парадными воротами Запретного города и самым высоким сооружением в императорском дворце. Максимальная высота его – 38 м. На верхней части ворот Умэнь, на арке расположена башня. По обеим ее сторонам на уголках стоят четыре высокие беседки. Эти пять построек напоминают птиц, готовых вот-вот взлететь. Поэтому ворота Умэнь еще называют "Башней пяти фениксов". В прошлом здесь часто устраивались официальные торжества.

琉璃雕花
A glazed ornament in the Forbidden City
Fleurs en verre colorée sculptées
Dekorationsornament aus Farbglasur (Qing-Dynastie)
Резьба из глазуря

角楼是城池的一部分，也起着防护作用。角楼结构精巧复杂，十字形屋脊，多角交错，其中沿城墙延伸的两面比城墙外端的两面稍长，这样就增强了城上建筑的稳固之感。

Corner Tower【英文】As a major component of the city structure, the corner tower has strong defensive effects. It's covered with a cross-shaped roof, with interlacing corners. Two sides extending along the wall are a little longer than the wall, hence strengthening the sense of steadiness.

Tours d'angles【法文】Faisant partie des remparts, les tours d'angles jouaient aussi un rôle défensif. Les tours d'angles présentent une structure ingénieuse et complexe, les faîtes en forme de croix et les angles s'entrecroisant. Pour les tours, les deux parties qui s'étendent le long de la muraille sont plus longues que les deux autres, ce qui permet de donner le sentiment de stabilité aux constructions sur la muraille.

Ecktürme【德文】Die vier Ecktürme dienten nicht nur als Schützanlage der Stadtmauer, sondern auch als Dekoration der Stadtmauer. Von weitem gesehen sieht jeder Eckturm wie ein prächtiger Pavillon mit einem dreifachen Kegeldach aus.

Угловая башня【俄文】Угловая башня – частью системы обороны Запретного города. Конструкция угловой башни сложна и уникальная. Конек ее крыши – в форме креста. Длина двух сторон башни, протянувших вдоль стены, больше той остальных сторон башни, стоящих внутри стены.

神武门为紫禁城的北门，是后妃或皇室人员出入皇宫的专用门。清代选秀女时，秀女们要由神武门进入宫中候选。1924年溥仪由此门被逐出宫。现在，作为故宫的临时展览场所，小型展览经常在此展出。

Gate of Martial Spirit【英文】As the north gate of the Forbidden City, the Gate of Martial Spirit was particularly for imperial concubines and members to come in and go out of the imperial palace. In the Qing Dynasty, the girls went into the Forbidden City to be selected as maids or concubines through this gate, and in 1924 the last Qing emperor Puyi (r. 1908-1911) was driven out of the Forbidden City from this gate. Now, the Gate of Martial Spirit was worked as the temporary site for small-scale exhibitions.

Porte de la Prouesse divin【法文】La Porte de la Prouesse divine, qui est le passage nord de la Cité interdite, était réservée aux concubines et à d'autres membres de la famille impériale. Sous la dynastie des Qing, les filles sélectionnées devaient entrer dans le Palais à travers la Porte de la Prouesse divine, afin d'attendre les sélections suivantes. En 1924, le dernier empereur des Qing a été expulsé du Palais par cette porte. Désormais, des petites expositions ont lieu souvent dans cette porte.

Das Shenwumen-Tor【德文】Das Shenwumen-Tor ist der nördliche Eingang des Kaiserpalastes, der früher für die Konkubinen des Kaisers und seine anderen Familienangehörigen bestimmt war. In der Qing-Zeit gingen die Kandidatinnen der Konkubinen des Kaisers durch dieses Tor in den Kaiserhof. Im Jahre 1924 wurde der letzte Qing-Kaiser Pu Yi durch dieses Tor aus dem Kaiserhof vertrieben. Heute dient das Shenwumen-Tor als Haupteingang des Palastmuseums.

Шэньумэнь【俄文】Ворота Шэньумэнь являются северными воротами Запретного города и специальным входом для императриц, наложниц или членов императорской семьи. В 1924 г. Пу И, последний император династии Цин, был выгнан из дворца через эти ворота. Теперь они служат местом для проведения временных выставок.

Cour extérieure Der Außenhof Внутренние павильоны

OUTER COURT

外朝 OUTER COURT

Cour extérieure Der Außenhof
Внутренние павильоны

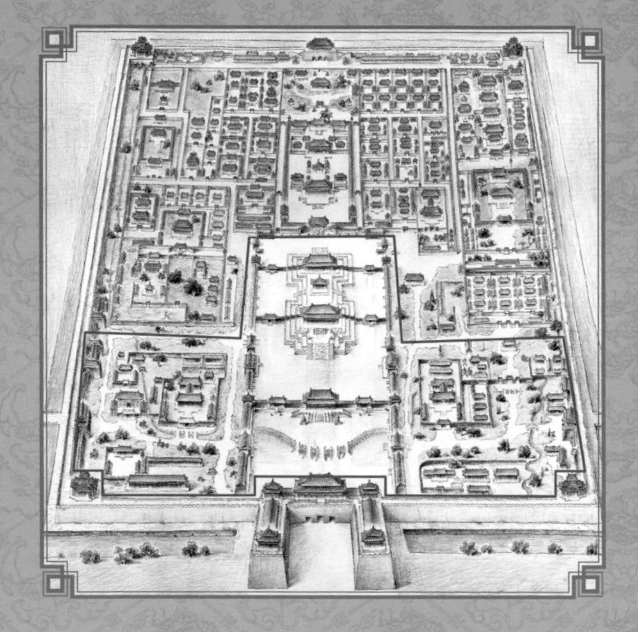

外朝：

外朝的主体建筑为三大殿，即太和殿、中和殿和保和殿，又称“前三殿”，是皇帝举行大典、召见群臣和行使权力的地方。三大殿是皇权和威严的象征，因此居于宫城的中心位置，占地最广。

Outer Court【英文】The Outer Court is centered on Three Grand Halls, namely, Hall of Supreme Harmony, Hall of Middle Harmony, and Hall of Preserving Harmony, together also called “Three Front Halls”. The three halls were where emperors held grand ceremonies, summoned ministers and wielded power, symbolizing imperial power and dignity. Thus they stand in the center of the Forbidden City and occupy the largest area.

Cour extérieure【法文】La Cour extérieure abrite principalement trois salles : la salle de l'Harmonie Suprême, la salle de l'Harmonie Parfaite et la salle de l'Harmonie Préservée, appelées aussi « salles antérieures ». C'était là où l'empereur présidait des grandes cérémonies officielles, recevait ses ministres et exerçait son pouvoir. Les trois salles, symbols de l'autorité et la dignité impériales, se trouvent au centre de la Cour extérieure et occupent une place plus grande que les autres constructions.

Der Außenhof【德文】Der Außenhof mit den drei Haupthallen Taihedian (Halle der Höchsten Harmonie), Zhonghedian (Halle der Vollkommenen Harmonie) und Baohedian (Haller der Erhaltung der Harmonie) als Mittelpunkt liegt im Süden des Kaiserpalastes. Hier emping der Kaiser seine Minister, übte seine Macht aus und hielt wichtige Feiern und große Zeremonien ab.

Внутренние павильоны【俄文】Главными сооружениями внешних павильонов – павильоны Тайхэдянь, Чжунхэдянь и Баохэдянь, которые предназначались для проведения важнейших государственных и придворных церемониалов. Они – символ императорской власти, поэтому находятся в центре Запретного города и занимают крупнейшую площадь в нем.

金宗喀巴像
A gold statue of Tsong-kha-pa
Figure d'un bouddha
Goldstatue von Tsong-kha-pa
Золотая статуя Цзокаба

内金水河

内金水河在紫禁城内蜿蜒2000多米，其形状宛如玉带，因此又被称为“玉带河”。它为宫中防火提供了充足的水源，还兼起到排泄雨水和装点广场的作用。新中国成立后，内金水河河道几经清理，河岸多次被加固和整修。

The Inner Golden Water River【英文】The Inner Golden Water River wanders 2,000 meters in the Forbidden City like a jade ribbon, thus called Jade Ribbon River. It has the functions of supplying water source for fire prevention, draining off the rain, decorating the square, and etc. Since the founding of the People's Republic of China, the river course has been cleared and improved, and the bank reinforced and rebuilt.

Rivière intérieure aux Eaux d'or【法文】La rivière intérieure aux Eaux d'or s'étend sur 2 000 mètres dans la Cité interdite, comme une ceinture de jade, appelée aussi « Rivière Yudai (ceinture de jade) ». Cette rivière approvisionne la Cité en eau pour la prévention des incendies, tout en jouant le rôle de l'évacuation des eaux de pluie et de la décoration. Depuis la fondation de la Chine nouvelle, le cours d'eau a connu plusieurs draguages et les rives ont été aussi restaurées et consolidées.

Der Innerne Goldwasser-Fluss【德文】Es handelt sich dabei um einen 2000 m langen Kanal innerhalb des Außenhofes. Dieser Kanal sieht wie ein Jadegürtel aus und wird auch Jadegürtel-Fluss genannt. Er war früher für die Feuerbekämpfung und Entwässerung innerhalb des Kaiserpalastes von großer Bedeutung. Nach der Gründung der Volksrepublik China wurde dieser Kanal mehrmals ausgebaggert.

Канал Нэйцзиньшуйхэ【俄文】Канал Нэйцзиньшуйхэ протягивается на 2000 м. в Запретном городе. Форма его напоминает нефритовый пояс, поэтому еще называется Юйдайхэ (река нефритового пояса). Он не только предоставляет достаточную воду для предупреждения пожара во дворце, но и помогает отведению воды и украшает площадь.

画珐琅开光梅花纹鼻烟壶
A Qing Dynasty painted enameled snuff bottle with the pattern of plum blossoms
Pot en émail à dessins de fleurs et du caractère Longévité, datant des Qing
Emailenkrug mit Blumenmustern und chineischen Schriftzeichen „Shou" (Qing-Dynastie)
Эмалевый чайник с узорами цветов и иероглифа «寿» (династия Цин)

画珐琅花卉寿字纹卤壶（清）
A Qing Dynasty painted enameled pot with the patterns of flowers and the Chinese character of "shou"
Pot en émail à dessins de fleurs et du caractère de Longévité, datant des Qing
Emailenkrug mit Blumenmustern und chinesischen Schriftzeichen „Shou" (Qing-Dynastie)
Эмалевый чайник с узорами цветов и иероглифа «寿» (династия Цин)

广场位于太和门前，占地26000平方米，广场南端有五架并排的内金水桥。正中的御路桥长23.5米，宽6米，是紫禁城中最有气魄的一座桥，为皇帝行走专用。王公大臣们行走两侧的四座桥。桥下的内金水河蜿蜒流淌。举目北望，太和门居中，昭德门和贞度门分立其东西。广场两侧是东西廊庑，居于中心位置的协和门和熙和门东西对峙。东廊庑在明代用作实录馆、玉牒馆和记载皇帝每日活动的起居注馆，清代时是稽查钦奉上谕处和内阁制敕房两个枢密机构的所在地；西廊庑在明代是编修《大明会典》的会典馆，在清代则改为起居注馆和掌满汉文对译的翻书房。

Gate of Supreme Harmony Square 【英文】The Gate of Supreme Harmony Square lies in front of the Gate of Supreme Harmony, covering an area of 26,000 square meters. In the south of the square there are five Inner Golden Water Bridge. The middle path of the bridge, 23.5 meters long and six meters wide, is the most magnificent, which was exclusively for imperial use in the past. The four bridges beside it on both sides were for royal ministers. The Inner Golden Water River runs under the bridge. In the north of the square stands the Gate of Supreme Harmony flanked by Zhaode Gate and Zhendu Gate. There is a row of wing rooms respectively in the east and west sides of the square. The east rooms were used as halls to keep royal family trees and records about emperor's daily life in the Ming Dynasty, but the Privy Council in the Qing Dynasty. The west rooms were originally where records of laws and systems of dynasty were compiled in the Ming Dynasty and were altered into halls to keep records of emperor's daily life and translation center for Manchu and Chinese languages.

Place de la porte de l'Harmonie suprême 【法文】Se trouvant devant la porte de l' Harmonie suprême, la place couvre 26 000 m². Au sud de la place, sont les cinq ponts qui enjambent la rivière intérieure aux Eaux d'or, dont le central, le plus majestueux de la Cité interdite, était réservé à l'empereur, et les ponts à côté aux ministres. La rivière intérieure aux Eaux d'or au dessous des ponts serpente.

Der Taihemen-Platz 【德文】Der Taihemen-Platz liegt vor dem Taihemen-Tor und nimmt eine Fläche von 26 000 Quadratmetern ein. An seinem südlichen Rand sieht man über den Inneren Goldasser-Fluss fünf Bogenbrücken aus weißem Marmor. Die mittlere Brücke ist 23,5 m lang und 6 m breit. Früher war sie für den Kaiser bestimmt.

Площадь Тайхэмэнь 【俄文】Перед воротами Тайхэмэнь есть просторная площадь с названием Тайхэмэнь. Площадь занимает 26000 кв.м. На ей есть канал Нэйцзиньшуйхэ, через который переброшено пять мостов. Центральный мост длиной 23,5 м, шириной 6 м. был предназначен исключительно для императора и называется главным мостом. Остальные четыре моста были предназначены для князей и вельможей.

明黄缎平金彩乡龙皇帝朝袍（清）
The imperial robe worn by Qing emperors
Robe impériale en satin jaune de l'empereur, datant des Qing
Kaiserliches Gewand mit Drachenmustern (Qing-Dynastie)
Императорская парадная форма из желтого шелка с узорами дракона (династия Цин)

三羊尊（商）
A Shang Dynasty three-sheeped *Zun* (Wine Vessel)
Vase à trois chèvres datant des Shang
Sanyang-Zun, Bronzeweingefäß mit Mustern von drei Schafköpfen (Shang-Dynastie)
Бронзовый треножник с рельефами трех овцов (династия Шан)

太和门及门前铜狮

太和门为紫禁城内等级最高的门。明代皇帝在此"御门听政"。1644年，清顺治皇帝福临在这里登基，颁布诏书，大赦天下。此外，顺治帝加封多尔衮为摄政王、封吴三桂为平西王等活动也在太和门举行。明清时期，太和门屡遭大火焚毁，现今所见的太和门为清末光绪二十年（1894年）重建。太和门前的铜狮是紫禁城内最大的一对。左侧脚踩铜球的铜狮为雄，右侧脚抚幼狮的铜狮为雌。雄狮象征着一统天下，雌狮寓意子嗣昌盛。这对铜狮都是皇权至高无上的象征。

Gate of Supreme Harmony and Bronze Lions 【英文】The Gate of Supreme Harmony, the highest-ranking gate in the Forbidden City, was where the Ming emperors handled state affairs, listened to ministers' reports and issued imperial edicts. It witnessed Emperor Shunzhi's ascending the throne in 1644, Dorgon's promotion to the prince regent, and the surrender Ming general Wu Sangui's conferring of Prince Pingxi. It was burnt down for several times since completion, and the gate we see now was latest rebuilt in 1894, the 20th reign year of Emperor Guangxu. In front of the gate places a pair of bronze lions, the largest pair in the Forbidden City. The one on the left stepping on a ball is the male, while the one on the right touching an infant lion with its claw is the female. The male lion symbolizes dominant rule over the country and the fame represents multiplied descendants, both indicating emperor's supreme power.

Porte de l'Harmonie suprême et les deux lions de bronze 【法文】La porte de l'Harmonie suprême est au plus haut niveau de la hiérarchie dans la Cité interdite. Les empereurs de la dynastie des Ming « assistaient aux débats sur les affaires d'Etats devant cette porte impériale ». En 1644, Fulin, l'empereur Shunzhi de la dynastie des Qing y monta sur le trône. Les deux lions de bronze devant la porte représentent la plus grande paire de la Cité interdite. Le lion à gauche qui pose le pied sur une boule de bronze est mâle, celui à droite qui caresse un lionceau est femelle.

Das Taihemen-Tor 【德文】Das Taihemen-Tor wird auch das Tor der Höchsten Harmonie bezeichnet und ist das prächtigste Tor des Kaiserpalastes. Früher fanden hier wichtige Zeremonien statt. Im Jahre 1644 trat der Kaiser Fu Lin hier die Thronfolge an. Links und rechts vor dem Taihemen-Tor liegen zwei Bronzelöwen. Sie sind größten ihrer Art im Kaiserpalast. Die linke Löwenfigur ist männlich und die rechte weiblich.

Ворота Тайхэмэнь и бронзовые львы 【俄文】По рангам ворота Тайхэмэнь занимают первое место среди других ворот Запретного города. В октябре 1644 г. здесь 6-летний император Шуньцзы вступил на трон. Бронзовые львы перед воротами Тайхэмэнь являются самыми большими бронзовыми львами в Запретном городе. Лев, под левой ногой которого есть бронзовый шарик – самец. Лев, под правой ногой лежит маленький лев – самка.

太和門

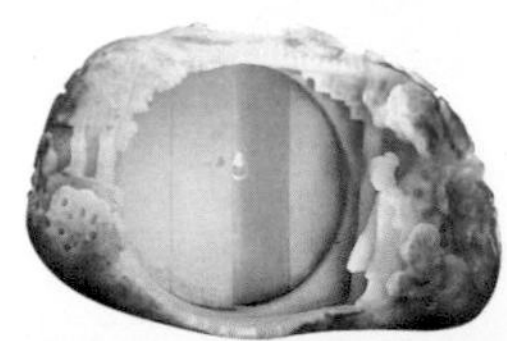

"桐荫仕女图"玉摆件（清）
A Qing Dynasty jade ornament
Objet de jade « Peinture représentant des beautés sous l'ombrage des sterculiers à feuilles de platane », datant des Qing
„Hofdame im Baumschatten", Schmuckstück aus Jade (Qing-Dynastie)
Нефритовое изделие «девушка под деревом» (династия Цин)

体仁阁

体仁阁于明永乐十八年（1420年）建，明初称为"文楼"，清顺治二年（1645年）改名为"体仁阁"并沿用至今。体仁阁面阔九间，进深三间，庑殿式屋顶。清朝前期常在这里举行与考选文士有关的活动，清康熙时，博学鸿儒的考试在这里举行，后作为宫廷库房。

Pavilion of State Benevolence【英文】Built in the 18th year of Emperor Yongle's reign of Ming (1420) and originally named Civil Tower, the Pavilion of State Benevolence was renamed the present name in the second year of Emperor Shunzhi's reign (1645). The pavilion is nine bays wide and three bays deep, covered with a hip roof with one horizontal and four sloping ridges. It was used as the examination hall for literati during the early Qing Dynasty, especially during Emperor Kangxi's reign (1661-1722). Latcr, it was functioned as a storehouse.

Pavillon de la Manifestation de la Bienveillance (Tiren)【法文】Construit en 1420, à la 18e année du règne de l'empereur Yongle des Ming, fut appelé « Wenlou » (Pavillon des lettrés) au début de l'époque des Ming. En 1645, à la 2e année du règne de l'empereur Shunzhi des Qing, il fut baptisé « Tiren Ge ». Ce pavillon au toit à cinq faîtes comprend horizontalement neuf pièces et verticalement trois. Au premier temps de la dynastie des Qing, des examens pour les lettrés y furent souvent organisés. Par la suite, il serva d'entrepôt du Palais impérial.

Die Tirenge-Halle【德文】Die Tirenge-Halle, am östlichen Rand des Taihedian-Platzes gelegen, wurde im 18. Jahr (1420) der Yongle-Regierungsperiode der Ming-Dynastie erbaut. Diese Halle mit einem Walmdach hat eine Länge von 9 Räumen und eine Breite von 3 Räumen. Anfangs hiss sie Wenlou. Ihr heutige Name stammt aus dem 2. Jahr (1645) der Shunzhi-Regierungsperiode der Qing-Dynastie. Am Anfang der Qing-Dynastie wurden hier kaiserliche Prüfungen durchgeführt und diente später als Lageraum.

Терем Тижэньгэ【俄文】Находится на востоке площади Тайхэдянь. Был построен в 1420 г. В начале династии Мин носил название «Вэньлоу». В 1645 г., именно в династии Цин, был переименован в Тижэньгэ. При династии Цин здесь часто состоялись государственные экзамены. Потом он служил хранилищем дворца.

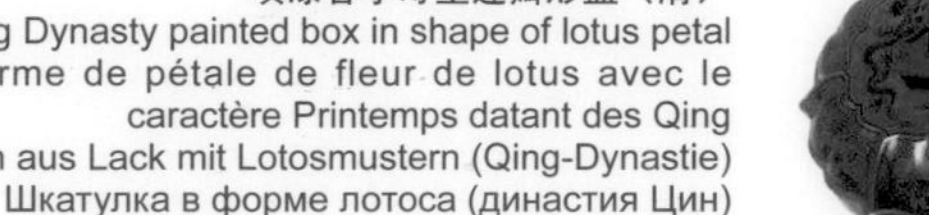

填漆春字寿星莲瓣形盒（清）
A Qing Dynasty painted box in shape of lotus petal
Boîte laquée en forme de pétale de fleur de lotus avec le caractère Printemps datant des Qing
Schmuckkästchen aus Lack mit Lotosmustern (Qing-Dynastie)
Шкатулка в форме лотоса (династия Цин)

弘义阁位于太和殿广场西侧，与体仁阁相对，在建筑形式和格局上与体仁阁一样，明初称为“武楼”，清顺治二年（1645年）改名为“弘义阁”并沿用至今。弘义阁曾为皇家的银库，专门收藏珍玩宝器、金银制线等。

Pavilion of Glorifying Righteousness【英文】Lying in the west of Hall of Supreme Harmony Square and opposite to Pavilion of State Benevolence, the Pavilion of Glorifying Righteousness has the same construction style and pattern as the Pavilion of State Benevolence. It was named Martial Tower in the Ming and renamed the present name in the second year of Emperor Shunzhi's reign (1645) in the Qing Dynasty. The pavilion was once used as the imperial treasury, mainly storing treasures, rare wares and gold and silver threads, etc.

Pavillon de la Grande Justice (Hongyi)【法文】Situé dans l'ouest de la place de la salle de l'Harmonie suprême, le pavillon de la Grande Justice est en face du pavillon de la Manifestation de la Bienvillance. Leurs forme architecturale et structures sont identiques. Au début de la dynastie des Ming, il fut appelé « pavillon militaire », et baptisé « pavillon Hongyi » à la 2e année du règne de l'empereur Shunzhi des Qing. En tant que Trésor impérial, le pavillon Hongyi était destiné à la conservation des bibelots précieux et des objets d'or et d' argent.

Die Hongyige-Halle【德文】Diese Halle liegt am westlichen Rand des Taihedian-Platzes. Sie ist so groß und prächtig wie die Tierenge-Halle. Anfangs hiss sie Wulou, ihr heutiger Name stammt ebenfalls aus dem 2. Jahr (1645) der Schunzhi-Reigerungsperiode der Qing-Dynastie. Sie diente als die Kaiserliche Kasse. Hier wurden Antiquitäten und Schätze sowie Gold- und Silbermünzen aufgewahrt.

Терем Хунъигэ【俄文】Находится на западе площади Тайхэдянь, напротив терема Тижэньгэ. По структуре и форме он с Тижэньгэ одинаковы. В первые годы династии Мин он носил название «Улоу». Потом в 1645 г. его переименовали в «Хунъигэ». Он был императорским казначейством, где хранились золотые, серебряные нити и многие драгоценности.

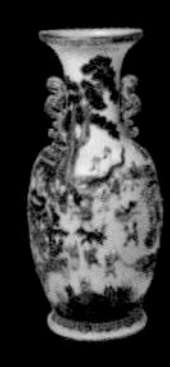

粉彩婴戏瓶（清）
A Qing Dynasty famille rose vase with the design of children at play
Vase émaillé mutlicolore à dessin de bébés datant des Qing
Blumenvase mit bemalten spielenden Kindern (Qing-Dynastie)
Фарфоровая ваза, покрытая картинкой «игра детей» (династия Цин)

三大殿基台

外朝三大殿均坐落于一座“土”字形三层基台上。每层台基四周都环以汉白玉石栏杆，栏杆下安有用于排水的石雕龙头，称为“螭首”。基台为汉白玉雕砌，高8.13米，台边高7.12米。三层基台间分列着鼎式香炉，平台上东边设日晷，西面陈嘉量，在日晷和嘉量的旁边还设有一对铜龟和铜鹤。

The Base of the Three Grand Halls 【英文】 The Three Grand Halls of the Outer Court are built on a three-tiered white-marble base, which takes a “土” shape. On four sides of the base are balusters, below which are thousands of stone-carved dragon heads used to drain water. In each dragon’s mouth there is a hole, through which water runs out. The base is totally 8.13 meters in height and 7.12 meters high on edges. Tripod-shaped incense burners spread on three tiers; the sundial and Jia Liang (a grain measure) are set oppositely to each other on the platform, with a pair of bronze tortoises and cranes by sides.

Terrasse des trois Salles 【法文】 Les trois Salles de la Cour extérieure sont situées chacune sur une terrasse à trois étages, en forme du caractère chinois « Tu ». A chaque étage, la terrasse entourée de la balustrade de marbre blanc, au dessous de laquelle des têtes de dragon sculptées en pierres, destinées à l’écoulement, appelées « Chi Shou ». La terrasse a une hauteur de 7,12 mètres, et avec la balustrade, celle de 8,13. Entre les trois étages se dressent des brûle-parfums de trépied. Sur la terrasse se trouve un cadran solaire dans l’est, et une mesure à grains dans l’autre côté.

Das „土“ förmige Postament der drei Haupthallen 【德文】 Die drei Haupthallen im Außenhof liegen auf einem 8,13 m hohen, „土“ förmigen und dreistüfigen Postament, das von Marmorbalustraden umgeschlossen ist. Unter diesen Balustraden sieht man viele Chishou- Steinschnitzereien (drachenförmige Steinschnitzereien). Auf dem Postament befinden sich 18 dreifüßige Weihrauchbehälter aus Bronze, ein Gnomon (Sonnenuhr) und ein Jialiang-Hohlmaß aus Bronze.

Платформа 【俄文】 Павильоны Тайхэдянь, Чжунхэдянь и Баохэдянь расположены на трехъярусных платформах в форме «土». На каждом ярусе кругом стоят мраморные перила, под которыми установлены каменные Чишоу для водоотведения. Высота платформы – 8,13 м. На трех ярусах платформы и полу перед нее расставлены 18 бронзовых треножных курильниц. На востоке платформы стоит Жигуй (солнечные часы), на западе ее – Цзялян (эталонная мера объема).

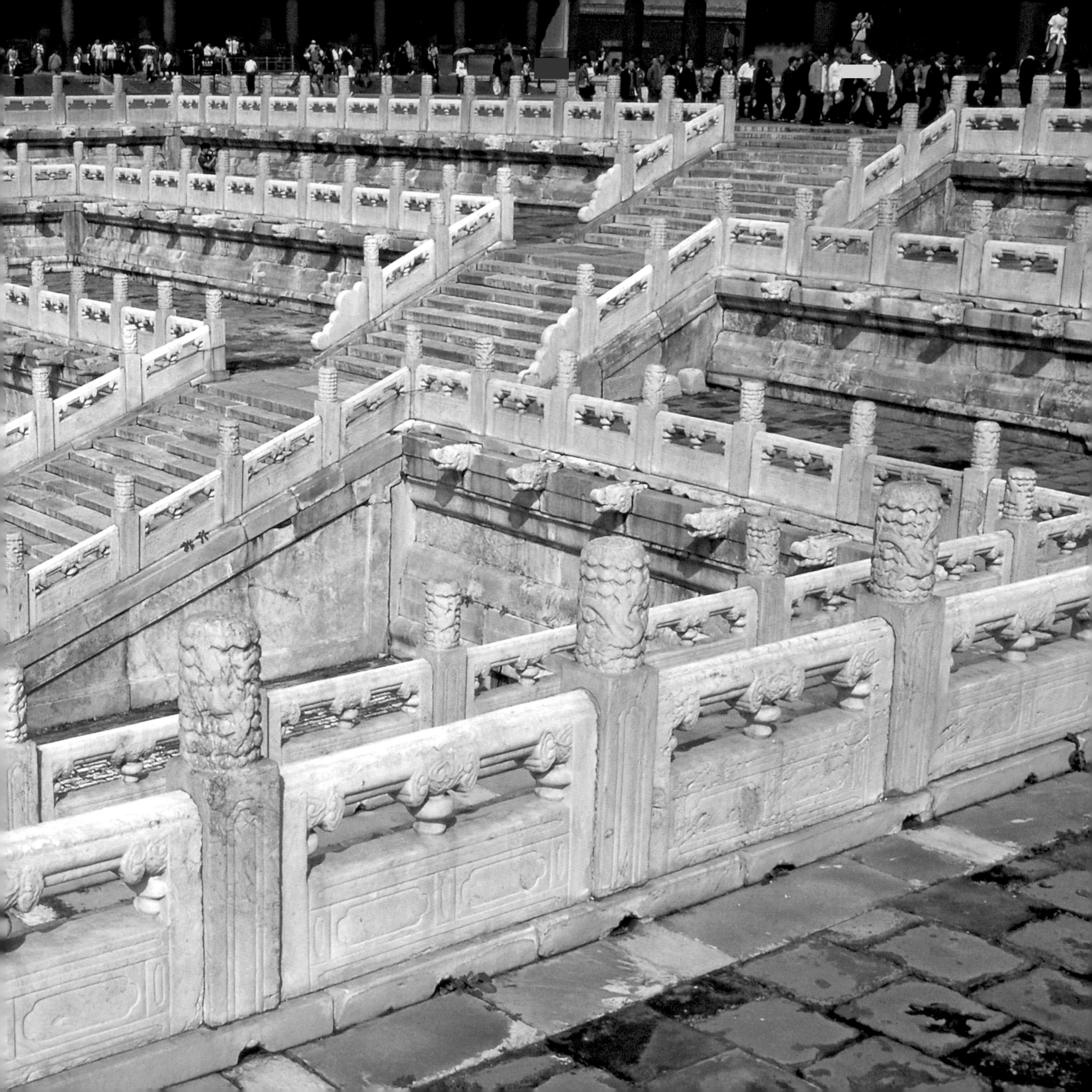

粉彩百鹿尊（清）
A Qing Dynasty famille rose vase with the design of thousands of deer
Vase émaillé multicolore à cent cerfs datant des Qing
Porzellanvase mit bemalten hundert Hirschen (Qing-Dynastie)
Фарфоровая ваза, покрытая картинкой «сто оленей» (династия Цин)

太和殿广场

太和殿广场为紫禁城内最大的广场，面积约3万平方米。明清举行大朝会时，广场中央甬道上陈列仪仗，文武百官东西站立。整个广场平坦宽阔，气势非凡，可容纳近7万人，显示出皇家的威严气魄。广场两侧各有一排以体仁阁和弘义阁为主体的廊房。

Hall of Supreme Harmony Square【英文】As the largest square in the Forbidden City, the Hall of Supreme Harmony Square occupies an area of around 30,000 square meters. On grand gatherings during the Ming and Qing dynasties, guards of honor carrying flags and weapons, etc. would stand in the middle path of the square, and civil and military courtiers stood beside the middle path. The broad and grand square can hold about 70,000 persons, revealing the imperial majesty and momentum. A row of side rooms separately centered on Pavilion of State Benevolence and Pavilion of Glorifying Righteousness stands on the east and west sides of the square.

Place de la salle de l'Harmonie suprême【法文】Avec une superficie de

文一品官服补子
An embodied attachment on the first-ranking Qing civil official's robes
Décoration de vêtement de l'officier civil de premier rang
Ornament eines Gewandes für hohe Beamte
«Буцзы» (квадратный кусок на парадной форме, символ разряда) на форме гражданского чиновника первой категории

30 000 m², cette place est la plus grande de la Cité interdite. Lors des audiences impériales dans les dynasties des Ming et des Qing, la garde d' honneur était sur le passage impérial au centre de la place, et les officiels civils et militaires se tenaient debout dans les deux côtés. Large et plate, cette place majestueuse peut contenir environ 70 000 personnes.

Der Taihedian-Platz 【德文】Der Taihedian-Platz liegt vor der Halle der Höchsten Harmonie. Mit einer Fläche von 30 000 Quadratmetern ist er der größte Platz innerhalb des Kaiserpalastes und kann 70 000 Menschen aufnehmen. Früher wurden hier wichtige Zeremonien veranstaltet, bei denen die Ehrengarde und alle Militär- und Zivilbeamten in der Rangfolge ihrer Dienstgrade vor dem Kaiser niederknieten.

Площадь Тайхэдянь 【俄文】Площадь Тайхэдянь – самая большая площадь в Запретном городе. Квадратная площадь занимает около 30000 кв. м. При династиях Мин и Цин император здесь принимал военных и придворных. Грандиозная и просторная площадь может вместить 70 тыс. человек.

御窑厂图瓶（清）
A Qing Dynasty painted vase
Vase peinte des Qing
Blumenvase (Qing-Dynastie)
Фарфоровая ваза, покрытая картинкой (династия Цин)

铜鹤
Bronze Crane
Grue de bronze
Bronzekranich
Бронзовый журавль

铜龟
Bronze Tortoise
Tortue de bronze
Bronzschildkrönte
Бронзовый черепах

龟和鹤是中国文化中的神灵动物，象征吉祥、长寿。

【英文】The tortoise and crane, the spiritualized animals in Chinese culture, symbolize luck and longevity.

【法文】La tortue et la grue sont des animaux divins dans la culture chinoise et symbolisent le bon augure et la longévité.

【德文】Diese Tierfiguren symolisieren das Glück und die Langlebigkeit.

【俄文】Черепах и журавль – священные животные в китайской культуре. Они – символ счастья и долголетия.

青花折枝花卉纹执壶（明）
A Ming Dynasty blue-and-white pot
Pot à dessins de fleurs datant des Ming
Weinkrug aus blau-weißem Porzellan (Ming-Dynastie)
Фарфоровый чайник с синим узором цветов на белом фоне (династия Мин)

日晷是中国古代发明的计时器，它利用太阳光照射指针投影到有刻度的石盘上以表示时间。

Sundial【英文】The sundial is a timepiece used in ancient China. Time is measured by means of a projection of the sun's shadow cast by the rod on the scaled plate.

Cadran solaire【法文】Etant un dispositif indiquant le temps, le cadran solaire montre les heures grâce aux ombres d'aiguilles créées par les rayons solaires sur le panneau de pierre.

Der Gnomon【德文】Der Gnomon ist ein antikes astronomisches Gerät und wird auch Sonnenuhr genannt.

Жигуй (солнечные часы)【俄文】Жигуй – прибор для определения времени по изменению длины тени от гномона и её движению по циферблату.

嘉量是中国古代的标准量器，上刻五级容量单位。这个嘉量是清乾隆时仿照王莽时期（9～23年）的嘉量形式制造的，器上刻有乾隆皇帝写的铭文。

Jia Liang【英文】Jia Liang was a popular measuring device, scaled five-level capacity units. This Jia Liang was made during Emperor Qianlong's reign (1735-1796), modeled on the one made during the reign of Wang Mang (9-23). The inscription on it was engraved by Emperor Qianlong.

Mesure à grains【法文】La mesure à grains est une mesure standard de l'antiquité chinoise et comprend cinq grades d'unité de contenance. Cette mesure à grains fabriquée durant le règne de l'empereur Qianlong des Qing était une reproduction de celle datant du règne de Wang Mang à l'époque des Han. L'inscription gravée sur la mesure fut écrite par l'empereur Qianlong.

Das Jialiang-Hohlmaß【德文】Bei dem Jialiang-Hohlmaß handelt es sich um ein Standardmeßgerät aus Bronze, das während der Regierungsperiode des Qing-Kaisers Qian Long nach dem Muster des Jialiang-Hohlmaßes aus der Regierungsperiode von Wang Mang der Han-Dynastie gegossen wurde.

Цзялян【俄文】Цзялян – эталонная мера объема в древнем Китае. На нем были вырезаны 5 единиц объема. Этот Цзялян был изготовлен при правлении цинского императора Цяньлун. На нем еще вырезана надпись, которую написал император Цяньлун.

红绿彩描金兽面纹镂空方薰（清）
A Qing Dynasty gilded vessel
Four aromatique ciselé à dessins d'animal des Qing
Räuchergefäß mit bemalten Tiermustern (Qing-Dynastie)
Квадратная печь с ажурной резьбой (династия Цин)

鼎式香炉

平台上陈列的18尊香炉，建造于清乾隆年间，是古代的一种礼器。皇帝举行大典时，在香炉内燃烧檀香和松枝，青烟升起时，为皇家大典增加一种庄严而神秘的气氛。香炉稳固的外形寓意江山、政权稳固。

Tripod-Shaped Incense Burners【英文】The 18 incense burners on the platform were built during Emperor Qianlong's reign, which were regarded as ancient important ritual wares. Whenever grand ceremonies were held, sandalwood and pine branches were burnt in the burners, which added a kind of stately and mysterious atmosphere to the imperial ceremonies with the rise of the smoke. The incense burners imply the stability and security of the power and state.

Brûle-parfum en forme de trépied【法文】Les 18 brûle-parfums s'étalant sur la terrasse, fabriqués durant le règne de l'empereur Qianlong des Qing, servaient d'objets rituels dans l'antiquité. Lors de grandes cérémonies présidées par l'empereur, des santals et des bois de pin y étaient brûlés. La fumée montante donnait une atmosphère solennelle et mystérieuse aux grandes cérémonies impériales. Le contour stable du brûle-parfum marque la stabilité du pays et du pouvoir.

18 dreifüßige Weihrauchbehälter aus Bronze【德文】Diese Weihrauchbehälter liegen auf dem Postament der drei Haupthallen. Sie wurden während der Regierungsperiode des Qing-Kaisers Qian Long gegossen und dienten als Ritualgeräte, die bei wichtigen Zeremonien benutzt wurden.

Бронзовые треножные курильницы【俄文】18 бронзовых треножных курильниц на платформе были вылиты при правлении цинского императора Цяньлун. Это ритуальный инструмент в древности Китая. Во время проведения церемонии в курильницах жгли сандаловое дерево и сосновые ветви. Дым, поднявшийся из них, добавил церемонии загадочность и грандиозность. Треножные курильницы – символ устойчивой власти.

螭首

螭是古代传说中一种没有角的龙，许多古代建筑都以其作为装饰。龙头口中含有小孔，每逢雨季，雨水自小孔中流出，呈现出千龙吐水的奇观，而基台上却不会淤积雨水。

Hornless Dragon Heads【英文】The hornless dragon, a legendary spirit, was used as the decorative pattern of many buildings in ancient times. In the rainy season, there is a wonderful scene of water running out of thousands of dragon heads, thus the base couldn't be filled with water.

« Chi Shou » (Tête de dragon légendaire)【法文】Chi est un dragon légendaire sans cornes et sert de décoration à de nombreuses constructions anciennes. Pendant la saison pluviale, les eaux de pluie s'écoulent de petits trous abrités par les têtes de dragons, de sorte qu'une scène « Les dragons jettent de l'eau » se présente. De plus, les eaux de pluie ne se déposent pas sur la terrasse.

Chishou-Steinschnitzereien【德文】Diese Steinschitzereien dienen nicht nur als Dekration für antike Bauten, sondern auch als Entwässerungsanlagen. Bei der Regenzeit fließt das Regenwasser aus dem „Drachenmund" hinunter.

Чишоу (голова дракона)【俄文】Чи – дракон без рогов в легендс. Многие древние сооружения украшаются им. Во рту дракона есть отверстие, через которое течет дождь. Таким образом, когда идет дождь, на платформе не будет стоячей воды.

"皇帝奉天之宝"（清）
An imperial seal of Emperor Qianlong of Qing
Sceau impérial de l'empereur Qianlong des Qing
Kaisersiegel aus Jaspis (Qing-Dynastie)
Яшмовая печать императора (династия Цин)

太和殿是紫禁城中等级最高的建筑。明清时，皇帝登基、大婚、册封、命将出征等大典以及万寿（皇帝的生日）、元旦和冬至三大节的大朝仪都在太和殿举行。清朝初期，殿试也在此举行。

Hall of Supreme Harmony【英文】The Hall of Supreme Harmony, the most magnificent in the Forbidden City, was where grand ceremonies like emperor's enthronement, imperial wedding and title conferring took place. It also witnessed royal banquets granted by emperor on his birthday, New Year's Day and Winter Solstice, as well as Final Imperial Examination held in the early Qing.

Salle de l'Harmonie suprême【法文】Surnommée « salle du trône », la salle de l'Harmonie suprême a l'échelon le plus haut de la Cité interdite selon la hiérarchie et est aussi l'édifice en bois le plus grand existant de nos jours en Chine. Sous les dynasties des Ming et des Qing, des grandes cérémonies avaient lieu dans cette salle. Par ailleurs, lors de l'anniversaire de l'empereur, du Nouvel An, du solstice d'hiver, l'empereur y recevait des félicitations des officiels civils et militaires et leur offrait un banquet.

Die Taihedian (Halle der Höchsten Harmonie)【德文】Die Taihedian, auch der Goldene Thronsaal genannt, ist die wichtigste der drei Haupthallen des Kaiserpalastes und auch der größte Holzbau Chinas. Von hier aus übte der Kaiser seine Macht aus. Viele wichtige Zeremonien wie die Zeremonie einer Thronbesteigung und die Audienzen für die Minister fanden hier statt. Zur Feier seines Geburtstages, des Neujahrs und des Dongzhi-Festes gab der Kaiser hier seinen Minstern ein Bankett. Anfang der Qing-Dynastie wurden kaiserliche Prüfungen in dieser Halle durchgeführt.

Павильон Тайхэдянь【俄文】Еще называется «Цзиньлуаньдянь». Это сооружение высшего ранга в Запретном городе, и крупнейший из сохранившихся деревянных павильонов в Китае. При династиях Мин и Цин здесь часто устраивались крупные церемонии, как вступление императора на трон, свадьба, присвоение титула. Каждый год в день рождения императора, Новый год и зимнее солнцестояние император здесь принимали поздравления от военных и придворных и устраивали банкет для них. В начале династии Цин дворцовые экзамены тоже проводились в Тайхэдяне.

建極綏猷
天心佑夫一德永
帝命式于九圍茲惟

粉彩帽筒
A Qing Dynasty famille rose decoration
Pot à chapeau émaillé multicolore
Porzellanbecher aus Famille rose
Фарфоровая коробка для шапок

太和殿内装饰金碧辉煌。金龙宝座居中，后有金漆屏风，两侧立6根蟠龙金柱，并陈设宝象、甪端、仙鹤和香亭，宝象象征国家的安定和政权的巩固；甪端是传说中的吉祥动物；仙鹤象征长寿；香亭寓意江山稳固。殿顶中央有金龙衔宝珠藻井，宝珠为轩辕镜，寓意明君当朝。

The Interior Hall of Supreme Harmony 【英文】The Hall of Supreme Harmony is resplendent and magnificent inside. A gilded nine-dragon throne sits in the center, sided by six dragon-patterned and gold foil covered columns and with a gilded dragon-carving folding screen behind. On both sides of the throne are elephants for peace of the country and stability of rule, *luduan* (an auspicious animal), cranes for longevity and pavilion symbolizing the stability of the country. In the caisson of the middle roof there is a gold-carved dragon, holding a pearl in the mouth. The pearl is called Xuanyuan Mirror, meaning that an enlightened emperor is on the power.

L'intérieur de la salle de l'Harmonie suprême 【法文】L'intérieur de la salle de l'Harmonie suprême est resplendissant de dorures : le sol pavé de briques dorées, les six colonnes dorées à motifs de dragon, la terrasse de nanmu doré sur laquelle le trône à motif de dragon et le paravent doré. Dans les deux côtés du trône se trouvent des objets en forme de l'éléphant, de l'animal légendaire « Luduan », de la grue et un kiosque parfumé. L' « éléphant » symbolise la stabilité du pays et un pouvoir consolidé ; « Luduan » est un animal légendaire de bon augure ; la grue marque la longévité ; le kiosque parfumé, le pouvoir stable. Dans le caisson au centre du plafond, un dragon d'or se couche et tient dans sa bouche une perle précieuse, qui est un miroir permettant de chasser les mauvais génies. Cela marque un bon empereur au pouvoir.

Innenansicht der Taihedian 【德文】Der Thron, in der Mitte dieser prächtigen Halle gelegen und von 6 mit goldlackierten Drachenfiguren dekorierten Säulen flankiert, steht auf einer Plattform aus Nanmu-Holz, die ebenfalls mit Drachfiguren verziert ist. Das Drachen-Pult und der Thronsessel sind mit geschnitzen Drachen- und Wolkenmustern stilisiert. Hinter dem Thron steht ein fein geschnitzter Wandschirm, vor und seitlich davon befinden sich Bronzefiguren von Kranichen, Elefanten und dem Fabeltier Luduan sowie Weihrauchgefäße. Über dem Thron befindet sich eine fein und kunstvoll gearbeitete Deckendekoration mit Drachenfiguren.

Интерьер Тайхэдяни 【俄文】Интерьер павильона блестящ и великолепен. В центре ее – шесть позолоченных колонн с изображением дракона. На постаменте из махила установлен трон с изображением дракона и ширма, покрытая золотым лаком. Перед ними стоят изящные бронзовые слоны, лудуань (святой зверь), журавли и треножные сосуды. Слоны символизируют спокойствие государства. Лудуань – символ счастья. Журавли – символ долголетия. Медные треножные сосуды – символ трона. Над троном золотой кессон с изображением дракона, во рту которого есть жемчуг.

太和殿门饰
Decorative Door of the Hall of Supreme Harmony
Décoration de la porte de la salle de l'Harmonie suprême
Türdekoration der Taihedian
Украшение на двери павильона Тайхэдянь

规矩鸟兽纹镜（东汉）
An Eastern Han Dynasty bronze mirror
Miroir à dessins d'oiseau et d'animal datant des Han de l'Est
Bronzespiegel (Östliche Han-Dynastie)
Зеркало с узорами птиц и зверей (династия Восточная Хань)

中和殿，方檐，渗金圆顶，如同一座华盖，因而明朝初建成时被称为“华盖殿”。中和殿的作用相当于太和殿的辅殿，皇帝去太和殿参加大典之前，先来此殿休息并接受文武官员朝拜。

Hall of Middle Harmony 【英文】The Hall of Middle Harmony is covered with a square-eaved round roof, which is like a *hugai* (canopy), thus the hall was named Huagai Hall when it was completed in the early Ming Dynasty. The hall was served as a resting hall for emperors to rehearse ministers here before attending grand ceremonies held in the Hall of Supreme Harmony.

Salle de l'Harmonie parfaite 【法文】La salle de l'Harmonie parfaite, aux avant-toits carrés et au toit rond doré qui ressemble à une voûte, fut baptisée « salle Huagai (voûte) » au début de la dynastie des Ming. C'est là que l'empereur reposait et recevait les officiers avant une grande cérémonie tenue dans la salle de l'Harmonie suprême.

Die Zhonghedian (Halle der Vollkommenen Harmonie) 【德文】Dieses Bauwerk hat die Form einer rechteckigen Gartenlaube. Bevor sich der Kaiser in die Thronhalle begab, ruhte er sich hier aus und empfing seine Minister in Audienz oder ließ die Zeremonien proben.

Павильон Чжунхэдянь 【俄文】Квадратный павильон Чжунхэдянь позади Тайхэдянь является местом, где император отдыхал и дал аудиенции высшим гражданским и военным чинам до начала церемоний в Тайхэдянь. Крыша павильона напоминает хуагай (балдахин над императорской коляской). Поэтому в династии Мин он еще назывался павильоном Хуагайдянь.

填漆八角盒（清）
A Qing Dynasty lacquer octagonal box
Boîte en laque octogonale des Qing
Achteckiger Kasten aus Lack (Qing-Dynastie)
Восьмиугольная лаковая коробка (династия Цин)

中和殿是礼仪性大殿。在举行祭地、藉田、祭祀社稷、太庙等仪式前，皇帝在此阅视祝版。恭上皇太后徽号前，皇帝在此阅视奏书。明、清两朝初期，皇帝在此赐宴亲王或重臣。

The Interior of Hall of Middle Harmony【英文】Hall of Middle Harmony is a ceremonial hall. Prior to grand sacrificial occasions, the emperor came here to review ceremonial placards before his departure to Altar of the Earth, Altar of Land and Grain, Imperial Ancestral Temple, etc. It was also where the emperor read memorials about the empress dowager's title of honor and banquets to princes and important officials were held in the early Ming and Qing dynasties.

L'intérieur de la salle de l'Harmonie parfaite【法文】L'empereur lisait les éloges dans la salle de l'Harmonie parfaite, à la veille des cérémonies : sacrifice offert au sol, réquisition des champs, sacrifice au pays, sacrifices au temple des ancêtres de la famille impériale et au temple de Confucius. C'est aussi là que l'empereur lisait les rapports le jour avant d'attendre le titre d'honneur de l'impératrice douairière. Au début des Ming, l'empereur y accordait souvent un banquet aux princes. Au début des Qing, l'empereur Shunzhi y offrit aussi le banquet aux hauts officiers.

Innenansicht der Zhonghedian【德文】In dieser Halle gibt es auch einen Thron, einige Dreifüße und Weihrauchgefäße. Einen Tag vor der Verleihung des Ehtentitel für die Mutter des Kaisers oder vor den wichtigen Zeremonien überprüfte und genehmigte der Kaiser hier entsprechende Dokumente. Anfang der Ming-Dynastie gab der Kaiser oft hier den Fürsten und Herzögen ein Bankett. Der Qing-Kaiser Shun Zhi empfing seine Minister in Audienz und gab ihnen ein Bankett.

Интерьер Чжунхэдяни【俄文】За день до проведения церемоний император зашел к чтению пожеланий на доске в этом павильоне. В начале династии Мин император часто в Чжунхэдяни устраивал банкеты для принцев. В начале династии Цин император Шуньцзы отдельно устроил банкет для высших чинов.

斗彩如意耳蒜头瓶（清）
A Qing Dynasty overglaze colored vase
Vase à des oreilles en forme d'ail datant des Qing
Bunt glasierter Porzellanweinkrug (Qing-Dynastie)
Фарфоровая ваза с горлышком в форме чеснока (династия Цин)

中和殿与保和殿
Hall of Middle Harmony and Hall of Preserving Harmony
Die Zhonghedian und die Baohedian
Salle de l'Harmonie parfaite et Salle de l'Harmonie préservée
Павильоны Чжунхэдянь и Баохэдянь

保和殿

保和殿是三大殿中位置最北的一座。明朝时，保和殿是举行册立皇后、皇太子等大典时皇帝更衣的地方。清朝时，每年正月初一到十五，皇帝在此宴请各少数民族王公、亲王和文武大臣。此外，公主下嫁纳彩后，皇帝在此赐宴驸马、其父以及族中有官职的人。乾隆五十五年（1790年）以后，保和殿成为殿试的考场。此外，顺治和康熙两位皇帝都曾将此殿作为寝宫。

Hall of Preserving Harmony【英文】Standing at the northern point of the Three Grand Halls, Hall of Preserving Harmony was where Ming emperors robed before attending such grand ceremonies as determining the empress and crown prince. In the Qing Dynasty, from the first to fifth days of the first lunar month, the emperor hosted banquets to nobles and ministers of the minorities. After receiving the presents from the man's family during the princess' wedding, the emperor would give banquets to his son-in-law and his family members with official titles. Starting from 1790, the 55th year of Emperor Qianlong's reign, Final Imperial Examination began to be held here. In addition, it once functioned as the living quarters for Emperor Shunzhi and Qianlong of the Qing.

Salle de l'Harmonie préservée【法文】Parmi les trois salles de la Cour extérieure, la salle de l' Harmonie préservée est la salle la plus nord. Sous les Ming, c'est là que l'empereur changeait d' habits lors des cérémonies : conférer les titres de l'impératrice et du prince héritier. Sous les Qing, au 1er jour et au 15e jour du 1er mois lunaire, l' empereur y invitait à dîner les princes, ducs et ministres des ethnies minoritaires. Les banquets pour le mariage des princesses des Qing y furent aussi organisés. Après 1790 ans, soit à la 55e année du règne de l'empereur Qianlong, l'examen officiel présidé par l'empereur y fut organisé.

Die Baohedian (Halle der Erhaltung der Harmonie)【德文】Diese Halle ist die letzte der drei Hauptallen. In der Ming-Dynastie diente sie als ein Umkreidungsraum für den Kaiser vor verschiedenen Zeremonien. In der Qing-Dynastie gab der Kaiser alljährlich am 1. und 15. Tag des 1. Mondmonats den Fürsten und Herzögen aus nationalen Minderheiten ein Bankett. Zur Hochzeitfeier aller Prinzessinnen wurde hier ebenfalls ein Bankett veranstaltet. Seit dem 55. Jahr (1790) der Regierungsperiode des Kaisers Qian Long wurden hier kaiserliche Prüfungen durchgeführt.

Павильон Баохэдянь【俄文】Павильон Баохэдянь находится на севере к павильонам Тайхэдянь и Чжунхэдянь. Он был местом, где император переодевался до проведения церемоний. В династии Цин 1-го и 15-го января (по лунному календарю) каждого года император здесь устраивал банкет для князей и вельможей национальных меньшинств. С 1790 г. дворцовые экзамены начали проводиться в этом павильоне.

保和殿内景

保和殿内“金砖”铺地。镂雕金漆宝座坐北向南。宝座后为屏风，宝座上方和两侧分别悬挂乾隆皇帝题写的匾额和楹联。

The Interior of Hall of Preserving Harmony【英文】The Hall of Preserving Harmony is paved by “gold Bricks” (the costly bricks of completed and multiple processes). A gilded throne sits north and faces south, with a screen behind. The stele and a pair of couplets in the hall were written by Emperor Qianlong.

L'intérieur de la salle de l'Harmonie préservée【法文】La salle de l' Harmonie préservée abrite le trône et le parvant. Au dessus et sur les côtés du trône sont suspendus un panneau portant l'inscription et des sentences parallèles, toutes écrites par l'empereur Qianlong. Le sol est pavé de briques dorées et le trône doré et ciselé fait face au sud. L'empereur Shunzhi des Qing y habita dix ans, parce que le palais de la Puretée céleste était dans un état délabré après avoir connu la guerre. L'empereur Kangxi y habita aussi pendant huit ans.

Innenansicht der Baohedian【德文】In dieser Halle steht ebenfalls ein Thron und dahinter ein Wandschirm. Der Boden ist mit den Jinzhuan genannten rechteckigen Ziegelsteinen belegt. Über dem Thron sieht man eine horizontale Tafel mit einer vom Qing-Kaiser Qian Long geschriebenen Inschrift und an seinen beiden Seiten Spruchrollen, die ebenfalls vom Kaiser Qian Long geschrieben wurden. Der Qing-Kaiser Shun Zhi bestieg in dieser Halle den Kaiserthron und wohnte hier gut 10 Jahre. Der Qing-Kaiser Kang Xi lebte hier 8 Jahre.

Интерьер павильона Баохэдянь【俄文】В павильоне установлена ширма и трон, над которым висит доска с надписью императора Цяньлун. К тому же по бокам трона на колоннах есть парные надписи Цяньлуна. После вступления цинского императора Шуньцзы на престол он здесь прожил 10 лет. Дальше когда император Канси вступил на трон, он тоже здесь прожил 8 лет.

内廷 INNER COURT

Cour intérieure Der Innenhof
Внутренние резиденции

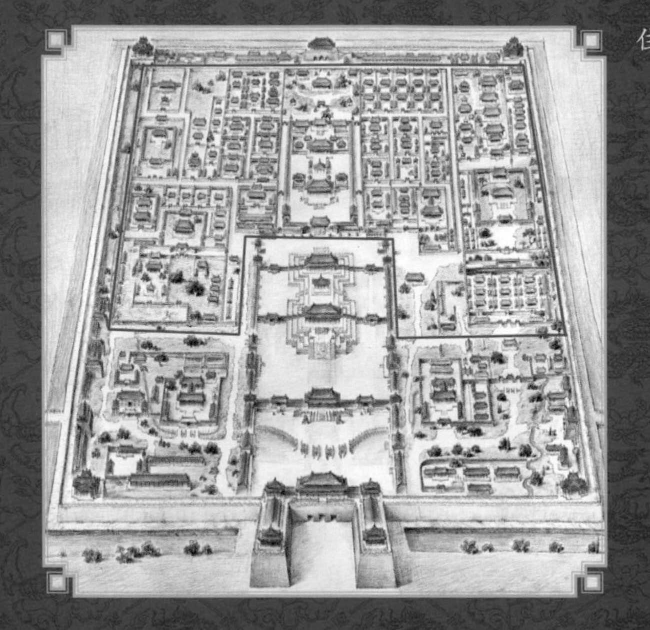

内廷：

内廷是皇帝及皇宫成员居住、游玩、奉神的地方，被视为“天地会合、阴阳交泰”之处。内廷以乾清宫、交泰殿、坤宁宫（统称后三宫）为中心建筑。后三宫两侧的东、西六宫，在明代是嫔妃们的居所，清代时后妃都可居住。

Inner Court【英文】The Inner Court, where the emperor and his extended family lived, enjoyed sceneries and worshipped the God, centers on Palace of Heavenly Purity, Hall of Union and Peace and Palace of Earthly Tranquility orderly in the axis line, commonly known as Three Back Palaces. On their left and right sides are Six Eastern Palaces and Six Western Palaces, where the Ming imperial concubines and the Qing empresses and concubines lived.

Cour intérieure【法文】La Cour intérieure, où l’empereur, l’impératrice et les concubines logeaient, se promenaient et offraient des sacrifices aux dieux, comprend principalement les trois palais postérieurs : le palais de la Pureté céleste, la salle de l’Union et le palais de la Tranquilité terrestre. Les palais de l’Est et de l’Ouest sur les côtés des trois palais postérieurs étaient réservés aux concubines sous les Ming et les Qing.

Der Innenhof【德文】Der Innenhof mit den drei Hauptpalästen Qianqinggong (Palast der Himmlichen Reinheit), Jiaotaidian (Halle der Berührung von Himmel und Erde) und Kunninggong (Palast der Irdischen Ruhe) als Mittelpunkt liegt hinter dem Außenhof. Zu seinen anderen Bauten gehören die sechs östlichen und die sechs westlichen Paläste. Hier lebte der Kaiser zusammen seinen Familienmitgliedern und erledigte laufende Staatsangelegenheiten.

Внутренние резиденции【俄文】Внутренние резиденции – это место, где императоры жили и занимались повседневными делами, жили и веселились их наложницы и дети. Павильоны Цяньцингун, Цзяотайдянь, Куньнингун являются главными сооружениями внутренней части. По обеим сторонам трех главных павильонов –шесть восточных и западных дворцов, где жили наложницы.

御制文津阁作歌扇子（清）
A Qing Dynasty fan
Eventail impérial datant des Qing
Fächer für Kaiser (Qing-Dynastie)
Веер для императора (династия Цин)

乾清门

乾清门是连接内廷与外朝往来的重要通道，在清代兼为皇帝处理政务的场所。门外两侧陈列的鎏金铜缸在明清时用于贮水防火。

Gate of Heavenly Purity【英文】The Gate of Heavenly Purity connects the Inner Court and the Outer Court. In the Qing Dynasty, it was served as an important place where the emperor handled state affairs. Several glazed copper vats flanked the gate were full of water to prevent from fire in the Ming and Qing dynasties.

Porte de la Pureté céleste【法文】C'est un passage important entre la Cour intérieure et la Cour extérieure et aussi un lieu où l'empereur traitait des affaires politiques. Les empereurs des Qing y assistaient aux débats sur les affaires d' Etat. Une paire de lions en bronze se dressent symétriquement devant la porte. Sur les côtés, il y deux jarres de bronze plaquées d'or. Sous les Ming et les Qing, elles étaient destinées à conserver de l'eau pour prévenir l'incendie.

Das Qianqingmen-Tor【德文】Es ist eine Demarkationslinie zwischen dem Außenhof und dem Innenhof. In der Qing-Zeit empfing der Kaiser hier seine Minister in Audienz und erledigte laufende staatliche Gelegenheiten. Vor dem Tor stehen zwei vergoldete Bronzelöwen und zu beiden Seiten davon mehrere ebenfalls vergoldene Wasserbehälter aus Bronze.

Ворота Цяньцинмэнь【俄文】Ворота Цяньцинмэнь – важный проход, связывающий внешние павильоны с внутренними резиденциями. Императоры Цинской династии принимали здесь официальные доклады. Тогда устраивался трон и начальники всех ведомств по очереди докладывали о своих делах. Перед воротами расставлена пара бронзовых львов и позолоченные медные чаны, которые хранили воду для огнетушения.

康熙皇帝朝服像

清朝皇帝大多勤理政事，而康熙皇帝的勤勉程度更在诸帝之上。康熙是清朝入关后的第二位皇帝，多才多艺，文韬武略兼备。从14岁亲政以后到去世之前，除因生病、三大节、重大变故外，康熙每天清晨都在乾清门前亲自主持御前朝廷会议，称作御门听政，一年四季从不间断。在康熙统治时期，清王朝由大乱走向大治，幅员辽阔、政治统一、经济繁荣，为“康乾盛世”的局面打下了基础。

Emperor Kangxi in Court Dress【英文】The Qing emperors were mostly diligent at state affairs, especially Emperor Kangxi (1654-1722). Kangxi, the second emperor after the Qing entered the Central Plains, was versatile, and proficient in civil administration and military strategy. Since his enthronement at the age of 14, Emperor Kangxi personally held the court every morning in front of the Gate of Heavenly Purity all year round, except for the conditions of illness, major festivals and sudden changes. During his reign, the Qing Dynasty earned wide territory, political unification and economical prosperity, which laid a solid foundation for the “Flourishing Age of Kangxi and Qianlong’s Reigns”.

Portrait de l’empereur Kangxi en habit impérial【法文】La plupart des empereurs des Qing furent assidus dans les affaires d’Etat et l’empereur Kangxi en fut le plus représentatif. Après avoir gouverné l’Etat par lui-même à 14 ans, Kangxi présidait personnellement le matin les réunions impériales devant la porte de la Pureté céleste, sans interruption pendant toute l’année.

Porträt von dem Qing-Kaiser Kang Xi【德文】Der Kaiser Kang Xi war einer der hervorragenden Herrscher der Qing-Dynastie. Im Alter von 14 Jahren bestieg er den Kaiserthron. Von da an stand er jeden Tag ganz früh auf und ging dann zum Qianqingmen-Tor, um seine Minister zu empfingen und staatliche Angelegenheiten zu erledigen.

Портрет императора Канси【俄文】Большинство цинских императоров прилежно занималось государственными делами. В этом аспекте император Канси превысил всех других. С 14 лет, когда он взял на себя бразды, Канси каждым утром у ворот Цяньцинмэнь принимал официальные доклады. Все время года такая работа не прерывалась.

象牙雕渔家乐图笔筒 （清）
A Qing Dynasty ivory carved pen container
Pot à pinceaux sculpté sur ivoire des Qing
Pinselbehälter aus Elfenbein (Qing-Dynastie)
Стаканчик для кистей с резьбой из слоновой кости, покрытый картинкой «веселый рыбак» (династия Цин)

乾清宫为内廷后三宫之首，坐落在单层汉白玉石基台之上。明代和清初，乾清宫是皇帝的寝宫，明朝的14位皇帝和清朝的顺治、康熙两位皇帝先后在此居住。清代时，乾清宫也是重要的典仪场所，千叟宴曾两次在此举行。自雍正将寝宫移居养心殿后，乾清宫成为正式引见官员及接待外国使臣的场所。此外，每逢辞旧迎新的时节，乾清宫被装点得灯火辉煌。

Palace of Heavenly Purity【英文】The major structure of the Inner Court, the Palace of Heavenly Purity sits on a single-tiered white marble base. In the Ming and early Qing dynasties, all 14 Ming emperors and two Qing emperors, Emperor Shunzhi and Kangxi, once lived in this hall. In the Qing Dynasty, the palace was an important political and ceremonious site, witnessing the Banquet for One Thousand Old Men held here twice. Since Emperor Yongzheng moved the residence to Hall of Mental Cultivation, Palace of Heavenly Purity became a formal place to receive officials and foreign envoys. On the New Year's festivals, the palace was brilliantly lit up and full of beauty.

Palais de la Pureté céleste【法文】Situé sur une terrasse de marbre blanc, le palais de la Pureté céleste est le premier des « trois palais postérieurs ». Dans cette chambre à coucher de l'empereur, 14 empereurs des Ming, les empereurs Shunzhi et Kangxi des Qing, habitèrent. Sous les Qing, le palais

任熊・《姚大梅诗意图》册（清）
A painting by Ren Xiong from the Qing Dynasty
Album de peintures poétiques réalisées par Ren Xiong des Qing
Malerei von Ren Xiong (Qing-Dynastie)
«Альбом живописи к стихам Яо Дамэя» Жэнь Сюна (династия Цин)

de la Pureté céleste fut aussi un lieu pour organiser des cérémonies. Deux banquets pour mille vieillards y furent organisés. Lors des fêtes dont le Nouvel An, le palais de la Pureté céleste était brillamment illuminé.

Der Qianqinggong (Palast der Himmlichen Reinheit)【德文】Der Qianqinggong ist der erste der drei Hauptpaläste im Innenhof. Er liegt auf einer Marmorterrasse und hat ein Doppeldach mit gelb glasierten Ziegeln. Dieser Palast diente als Schlafgemach für 14 Ming-Kaiser und für zwei Qing-Kaiser (Shun Zhi und Kang Xi). In der Qing-Zeit fanden hier auch wichtige Zeremonien statt. Das berühmte Qiansou-Bankett (Bankette für tausende Greise) wurde zweimal in diesem Palast veranstaltet.

Павильон Цяньцингун【俄文】Является главным павильоном внутренних резиденций. Расположен на мраморной платформе. При династии Мин и начале Цин это опочивальня императора. 14 минских императоров и цинские императоры Шуньцзы, Канси здесь жили. В династии Цин Цяньцингун – место, где часто проводились торжества. Здесь два раза устраивался «Пир для тысяч стариков».

紫红地粉彩楹竹梅纹题诗蟋蟀罐（清）
A Qing Dynasty cric ket pot
Pot à grillons en émail multicolore des Qing
Kasten zur Behaltung von Grillen (Qing-Dynastie)
Горшок для содержания сверчка (династия Цин)

坤宁宫

明代时，坤宁宫为皇后的寝宫。清顺治年间，仿照沈阳清宁宫对坤宁宫进行改建。改建后，坤宁宫的西暖阁用作宫内萨满教的祭祀场所，东暖阁被辟为皇帝举行大婚时的洞房。

Palace of Earthly Tranquility【英文】Originally the empresses' bedchamber in the Ming Dynasty, the Palace of Earthly Tranquility was rebuilt during Emperor Shunzhi's reign (1643-1661), modeled after the Palace of Pure Tranquility in Shenyang Imperial Palace. After rebuilt, the west chamber was served as the worshipping hall for Shamanism and the east one was used as the bridal chamber for the emperor's wedding.

Palais de la Tranquilité terrestre【法文】Sous les Ming, le palais de la Tranquilité terrestre était la résidence de l'impératrice. Durant le règne de l' empereur Shunzhi des Qing, il fut reconstruit à l'instar du palais de la paix et de la tranquilité à Shenyang. Après cette reconstruction, la chambre de l'ouest était réservée au culte de la religion Saman, et celle de l'est était la chambre nuptiale de l'empereur.

Der Kunninggong (Palast der Irdischen Ruhe)【德文】In der Ming-Zeit diente dieser Palast als Schlafgemach für die Kaiserinnen. Während der Qing-Zeit wurde er in zwei Teile gegliedert. Der westliche Teil mit dem Namen Xinuange als eine schamanistische Gebetshalle und der östliche Teil mit dem Namen Donginuange als Brautgemach für das Kaiserehepaar.

Павильон Куннингун【俄文】При минской династии здесь находилась опочивальня императрицы. При цинской династии этот дворец был реконструирован по маньчжурскому стилю. Западный флигель был реконструирован в священную камеру шаманизма. В восточном флигеле вы видите брачное ложе для новобрачных.

珍珠女朝帽（清）
A Qing Dynasty formal millinery inlaid peals
Chapeau à perles d'une femme se présentant à l'audience impériale des Qing
Phönixkrone, mit Perlen geschmuckt (Qing-Dynastie)
Женская шапка из жемчуга (династия Цин)

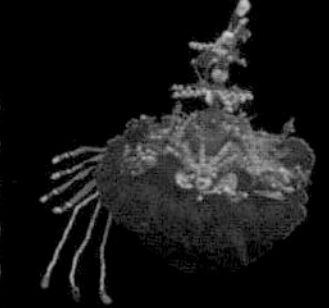

坤宁宫西暖阁内景

改建后的坤宁宫西暖阁是一处存放神亭、神像以及祭祀器皿的夹室。神堂内，北、西、南三面环成大炕形，届时祭祀时，炕上安放神像。凡遇大祭之日，皇帝、皇后都会亲来祭神。

The Interior of the West Chamber of the Palace of Earthly Tranquility 〔英文〕 The West Chamber was used to keep the statues and sacrificial containers. A *kang* was set with its north, south and west sides against the wall. On the day when the sacrificial ceremony was held, statues would be displayed on *kang* and the emperor and empress would come to worship the gods.

Chambre de l'ouest du palais de la Tranquilité terrestre 〔法文〕 TLa chambre de l'ouest du palais de la Tranquilité terrestre reconstruite était réservée à la conservation des statues de dieux et des ustensiles de culte. Sur le « kang » (lit de briques) de la salle divine, sont déposées des statues de dieux. Lors des grands jours de culte, l'empereur et l'impératrice y venaient personnellement faire des cultes aux dieux.

Innenansicht von Xinuange des Palastes der Irdischen Ruhe 〔德文〕 Xinuange ist auch der westliche Flügel des Palastes der Irdischen Ruhe und diente als eine schamanistische Gebetshalle. Hier fanden wichtige Religionszeremonien statt, bei denen das Kaiserehepaar immer anwesend war.

Интерьер западного флигеля павильона Куньнингун 〔俄文〕 Реконструированный западный флигель Куньнингуна – камера, где хранились статуя Божества и инструменты для жертвоприношения. Император и императрица часто сюда приходили и приносили жертвы божествам.

画珐琅五彩花鸟撇口瓶（清）
A Qing Dynasty painted enameled vase
Vase en émail multicolore à fleurs et oiseaux des Qing
Emailenvase mit bemalten Blumen- und Vogelmustern (Qing-Dynastie)
Эмалевая ваза, покрытая картинкой птицы и цветов (династия Цин)

清顺治、康熙、同治、光绪以及逊帝溥仪都曾在坤宁宫的东暖阁举行过大婚。现今东暖阁洞房内是光绪皇帝大婚时布置的原貌。屋内设有龙凤喜床、百子帷帐，四周墙壁上挂满祝福和吉祥画，整体陈列喜气满堂。

East Chamber of the Palace of Earthly Tranquility 〔英文〕In the Qing Dynasty, Emperor Shunzhi, Kangxi, Tongzhi, Guangxu and Puyi once held the wedding in this chamber. Now, the chamber keeps the original look of Emperor Guangxu's wedding. In the room sits a dragon-phoenix wedding bed (according to ancient belief, dragon symbolizes emperor while phoenix symbolizes empress). The bed curtain and silk quilt are embroidered with hundreds of playing children, meaning more children giving more blessings to the emperor and empress.

Chambre de l'est du palais de la Tranquilité terrestre 〔法文〕Les noces des empereurs Shunzhi, Kangxi, Tongzhi, Guangxu, ainsi que Puyi, furent organisées dans cette chambre. L'aménagement de la chambre de l'est est l' aspect original dans la noce de l'empereur Guangxu : le lit Dragon et Phénix, le rideau à Cent enfants, des peintures exprimant les félicitations et le bon augure sur le mur. Tous sont dans une atmosphère joyeuse.

Innenansicht von Dongnuange des Palastes der Irdischen Ruhe 〔德文〕Die vier Qing-Kaiser Shun Zhi, Kang Xi, Tong Zhi und Guang Xu sowie der abgedankte Kaiser Pu Yi feierten hier ihre Hochzeit. Das Brautgemach für das Kaiserehepaar Guang Xu ist heute noch original erhalten. Hier gibt es ein prächtiges Brautbett. Der Bettvorhang und das Bettzug sind jeweils mit hundert Kinderfiguren sls Symbol des Kindersegens verziert. An der Wand hängen viele glückverheißende Bilder.

Восточный флигель павильона Куньнингуна 〔俄文〕Здесь отмечалась свадьба трёх цинских императоров (Канси, Тунчжи и Гуансюй). Сегодня вы еще можете видеть, как расставлены вещи в этой комнате при свадьбе императора Гуансюй. Это кровать радости, шелковый полог с изображением ста детей, который символизирует многочисленное потомство императора, и т.д.

铜镀金点翠穿珠石九凤钿子（清）
A Qing Dynasty headwear for the female
Chapeau à neuf phénix des QingKopfschmuck (Qing-Dynastie)
Kopfschmuck (Qing-Dynastie)
Золоченные украшения с узорами девяти фениксов (династия Цин)

光绪皇帝大婚图

清代，皇帝大婚是一件大事。光绪十五年（1889年）正月，光绪帝的大婚典礼在紫禁城内举行。因为皇后是慈禧太后的亲侄女，婚礼耗资颇巨、豪奢隆重。大婚当日，宫内张灯结彩，举行奉迎和册立皇后等各种礼仪。两幅图分别描绘的是太和门内的迎亲队伍和太和殿前的迎亲喜轿。

Emperor Guangxu Getting Married (Partial) 【英文】In the Qing, the emperor's wedding is a magnificent event. In the first lunar month of 1889, Emperor Guangxu's wedding was held in the Forbidden City. As the future empress was Empress Dowager Cixi's niece, it cost a lot. The wedding is grand, luxurious, and sumptuous. On the wedding day, the whole palace was decorated with lanterns and colored hangings, and ceremonies including welcoming and determining the Empress were held. The two paintings separately illustrate the welcoming procession in front of Gate of Supreme Harmony and the bride's sedan chair in front of Hall of Supreme Harmony.

Tableau des noces de l'empereur Guangxu 【法文】 Sous les Qing, les noces de l'empereur furent un événement très important. Au jour des noces, le Palais impérial était décoré de lanternes et de festons. Des cérémonies solennelles étaient organisées : conférer le titre d'impératrice et accueillir la nouvelle impératrice.

„Die Hochzeit des Kaisers Guang Xu“ 【德文】Es handelt sich dabei um eine chinesische Malerei, die im Palastmuseum aufbewahrt wird. Sie zeigt, wie feierlich die Hochtzeit des Kaisers Guang Xu gehalten wurde.

Картина свадьбы императора Гуансюй 【俄文】При цинской династии свадьба императора – важное событие страны. В день свадьбы в Запретном городе украшались фонарями и шелком, устраивались торжественные церемонии.

五彩加金鹭鸶荷花纹凤尾尊（清）
A Qing Dynasty colored vessel with the pattern of bittern and lotus
Vase à dessins d'aigrette et de fleurs de lotus, datant des Qing
Vase mit bunt bemalten Lotosblumenmustern (Qing-Dynastie)
Фарфоровая ваза, покрытая картинкой лотосов и белой цапли (династия Цин)

后妃梳妆用具（清）
A toilet set of the Qing concubines
Ustensiles de toilette des impératrices et concubines datant des Qing
Toilettenartikel (Qing-Dynastie)
Инструменты для совершения туалета наложницами (династия Цин)

储秀宫

储秀宫为西六宫之一，清咸丰二年（1852年）慈禧刚进宫被封为兰贵人时，曾在这里居住，之后在这里生下同治皇帝。光绪十年（1884年）慈禧太后为庆祝50岁生日，重修储秀宫的宫室，并从长春宫移居于此。

Palace of Gathering Excellence【英文】As one of the Six Western Places, the Palace of Gathering Excellence was where Cixi, after being granted the title of Concubine Lan in the second year of Emperor Xianfeng's reign (1852), lived and gave birth to Emperor Tongzhi (r. 1861-1875). In the 10th year of Emperor Guangxu's reign (1884), to celebrate her 50th birthday, Cixi heavily renovated the palace before moving here from Palace of Lasting Spring.

Palais des Elégances accumulées【法文】L'un des six palais de l'Ouest, ce palais fut habité par Ci Xi, quand elle fut sélectionnée en 1852 (2e année de l'empereur Xianfeng des Qing) pour entrer dans le Palais et se fit conférer le titre de la concubine. Elle y donna naissance à l'empereur Tongzhi. En 1884, soit à la 10e année de l'empereur Guangxu, l'impératrice douairière Ci Xi fit reconstruire les chambres du palais des Elégances accumulées pour fêter son 50e anniversaire, et y déménagea du palais du Long Printemps.

Der Chuxiu-Palast 【德文】Der Chuxiu-Palast ist einer der sech westlichen Paläste. Von 1852 an lebte Ci Xi als Konkubine Lan des Qing-Kaisers Xian Feng in diesem Palast mehrere Jahre. Ihr Sohn Zai Chun, der sechs Jahre als Kaiser Tong Zhi den Thron bestieg, wurde hier geboren. Im Jahre 1884 wurde dieser Palast zur Feier des 50. Geburtstages der Kaiserinwitwe Ci Xi renoviert.

Павильон Чусюгун【俄文】Сзади павильона Янсиньдянь находится комплекс шести западных павильонов. В одном из этих павильонов, Чусюгун, жила одно время императрица Цы Си, когда она была еще наложницей. Дальше она здесь родила императора Тунчжи. В 1884 г. императрица Цы Си потратила 630 тыс. лян серебра на реконструкцию Чусюгуна, чтобы отметить свой 50-й день рождения.

御苑 IMPERIAL GARDENS

Jardins impériaux Kaiserliche Gartenanlagen Императорские сады

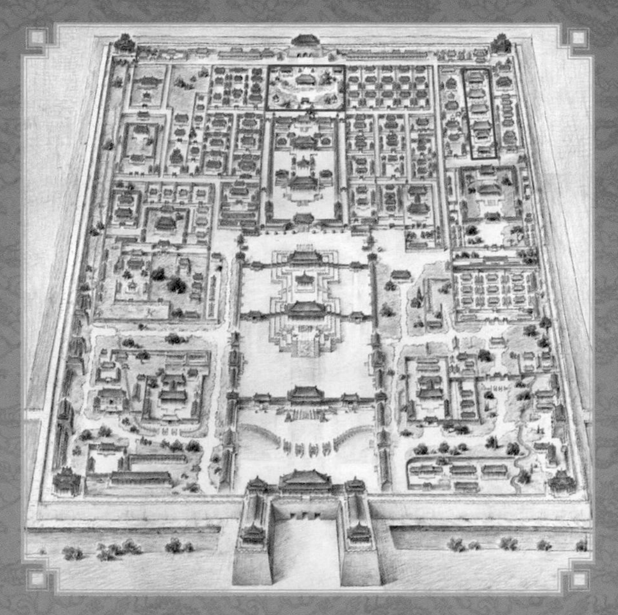

御苑：除了雄伟的宫殿、开阔的广场、精美的楼阁，紫禁城内还建有别具匠心的花园，如御花园，宁寿宫花园等，体现了封建宫城规划"前宫后苑"的布局。园里的怪石奇花，参天古木，楼台亭阁等景致错落随宜，使御苑既不失皇家园林的气派，又富有浓郁的园林特色。

Imperial Gardens【英文】Besides magnificent palaces, broad squares, exquisite pavilions, there are gardens of unique ingenuity in the Forbidden City, like the Imperial Garden, Qianlong's Garden, and so on, which is strictly in line with the layout of the feudal imperial palaces – palaces in the front and gardens at the rear. Additionally, wonder stones, exotic flowers, towering and old trees, towers and pavilions are all feasts for eyes, making the whole garden possessing the great imperial manner and the distinct garden features.

Jardins impériaux【法文】En plus des palais majestueux, des places larges et de belles tours, la Cité interdite abrite des jardins ingénieux, tels que le Jardin impérial, le jardin du palais de la Tranquilité et de la Longévité. Cela présente la disposition de la cité féodale marquée par « palais en avant et jardin en arrière ». Dans ces jardins, il y a des pierres étranges, fleurs rares, vieilles arbres imposants, pavillons, kiosques, etc.

Kaiserliche Gartenanlagen【德文】In der Purpurnen Verbotenen Stadt gibt es neben prächtigen Palästen und Hallen, weiten Plätzen und feinen Türmen auch einige Gartenanlagen wie den Palastgarten und den Ningshougong-Blumengarten. Hier sieht man seltene Blumen, künstliche Felsanlagen, uralte Bäume, Türme, Pavillons und Lauben.

Императорский парк【俄文】Кроме великоленного дворца, просторных площадей и изысканных теремов, в Запретном городе еще есть уникальные сады, как Юйхуаюнь (императорский сад), сад Ниншоугун. Изумительные цветы, причудливые камня, старые деревья, возвышающиеся до небес, уникальные сооружения придают императорским садам необычную красоту.

浮碧亭 Pavilion of Floating Green Pavillon Vert Flottant Der Fubi-Pavillon Беседка Фубитин

澄瑞亭 Pavilion of Pure Luck Pavillon Chengrui Der Chengrui-Pavillon Беседка Чэнжуйтин

御花园位于紫禁城中轴的尽头，是帝后嫔妃们游玩、休息的场所。御花园占地1.2万平方米，园内亭榭馆阁、殿堂，皆按主次相辅，东西对称的格局排列配置，其间点缀着苍松翠柏、奇花异木、水池叠石等。

粉彩百子图盘（清）
A Qing Dynasty famille rose plate
Assiette à peinture de Cent garçons en émail mutlicolore des Qing
Teller mit Mustern von hundert Kindern (Qing-Dynastie)
Фарфоровая тарелка, покрытая картинкой ста ребенок (династия Цин)

万春亭 Pavilion of Ten Thousand Spring Pavillon des Dix Mille Printemps Der Wanchun-Pavillon Беседка Ваньчуньтин

Imperial Garden 【英文】 The Imperial Garden, located at northern point of the axis line and covering a total area of 12,000 square meters, was a place of amusement for emperors, empresses and concubines. Pavilions and halls are distributed orderly, interspersed with pine trees, cypresses, and bamboos, as well as hills and rocks.

Jardin impérial 【法文】 Situé à l'extrémité de l'axe de la Cité interdite, le Jardin impérial est un lieu où l'empereur, l'impératrice, les concubines, s' amusaient et reposaient. En couvrant 12 000 m², il abrite des kiosques, pavillons, salles, qui sont tous arrangés de façon symétrique est-ouest. Ces constructions sont parsemées de pins, sapins, fleurs rares, étangs et pierres superposées.

Der Palastgarten 【德文】 Der Palastgarten liegt im Norden der Purpurnen Verbotenen Stadt und diente als Vergnügungspark für die Kaiser und ihre Frauen und Konkubinen. Auf einer Fläche von 12 000 m² sieht man hier uralte Kiefern und Zypressen, verschiedene Blumen und üppige Bambushaine, künstliche Felsanlagen, Pavillons und Lauben.

Юйхуаюань (Императорский сад) 【俄文】 В самой северной части Запретного города находится Императорский сад - Юйхуаюань. Здесь императоры с семьей и многочисленными наложницами веселились, любовались красотами природы. Общая площадь императорского сада—около 12000 квадратных метров. Он представляет собой образец садово-паркового искусства. На относительно небольшой территории архитекторам удалось создать ощущение значительного пространства.

紫禁城全景图

A panoramic view of the Forbidden City

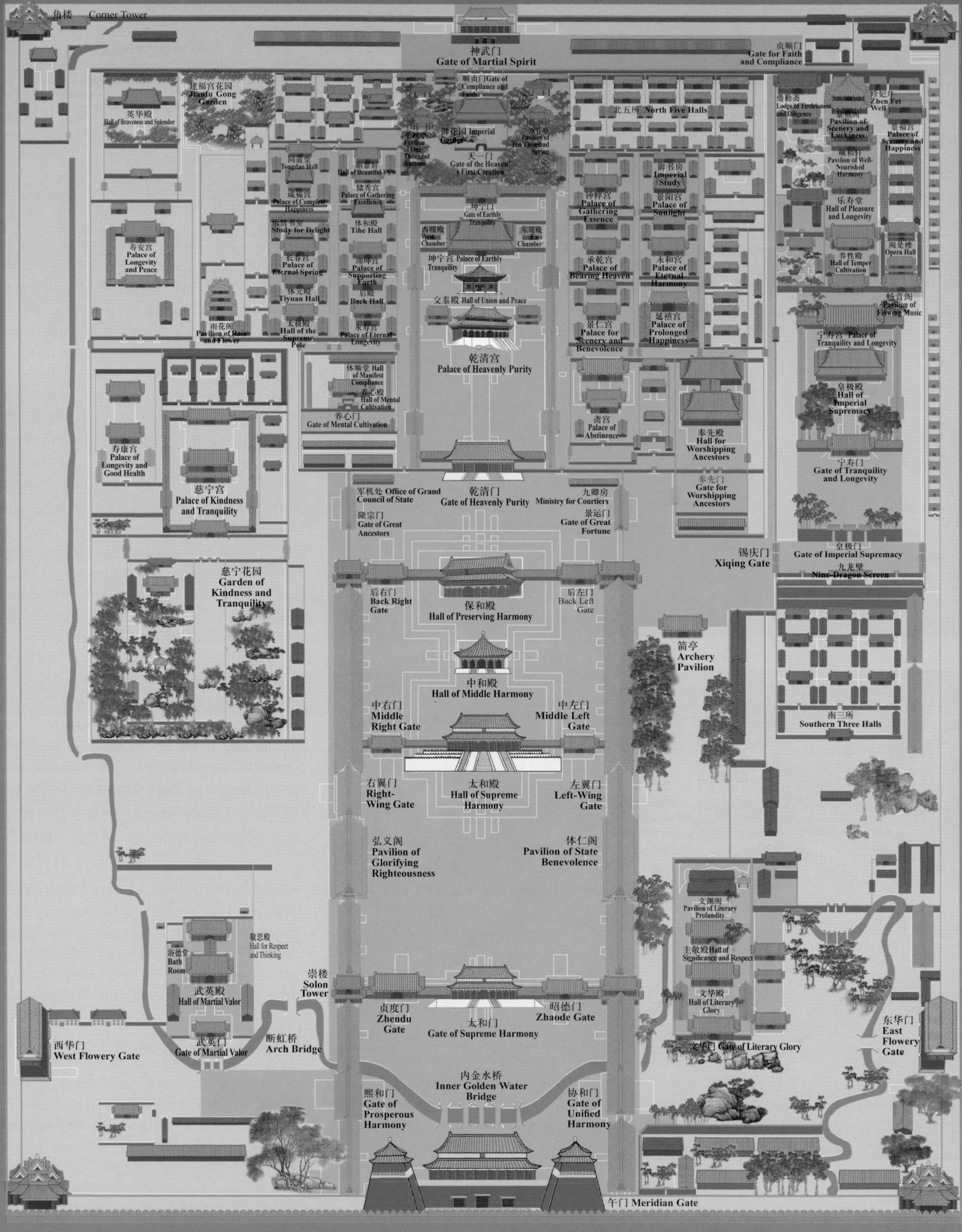

未开放区域 the unopened area
开放区域 the open area

角楼 Corner Tower
神武门
Gate of Martial Spirit
贞顺门
Gate for Faith and Compliance
筒子河 The Moat
英华殿
Hall of Braveness and Splendor
建福宫花园
Jianfu Gong Garden
顺贞门 Gate of Compliance and Faith
御花园 Imperial Garden
千秋亭 Pavilion of One Thousand Autumn
万春亭 Pavilion of Ten Thousand Spring
天一门
Gate of the Heaven's First Creation
北五所 North Five Halls
倦勤斋
Lodge of Tirelessness and Diligence
珍妃井
Zhen Fei Well
碧螺亭
Pavilion of Scenery and Luckiness
景祺阁
Palace of Scenery and Happiness
颐和轩
Pavilion of Well-Nourished Harmony
乐寿堂
Hall of Pleasure and Longevity
养性殿
Hall of Temper Cultivation
阅是楼
Opera Hall
畅音阁
Pavilion of Flowing Music
同道堂
Tongdao Hall
丽景轩
Hall of Beautiful View
咸福宫
Palace of Complete Happiness
储秀宫
Palace of Gathering Excellence
漱芳斋 Study for Delight
体和殿
Tihe Hall
长春宫
Palace of Eternal Spring
翊坤宫
Palace of Supporting Earth
体元殿
Tiyuan Hall
后殿
Back Hall
太极殿
Hall of the Supreme Pole
永寿宫
Palace of Eternal Longevity
雨花阁
Pavilion of Rain and Flower
寿安宫
Palace of Longevity and Peace
坤宁门
Gate of Earthly Tranquility
西暖阁
West Chamber
东暖阁
East Chamber
坤宁宫 Palace of Earthly Tranquility
交泰殿 Hall of Union and Peace
乾清宫
Palace of Heavenly Purity
钟粹宫
Palace of Gathering Essence
御书房
Imperial Study
景阳宫
Palace of Sunlight
承乾宫
Palace of Bearing Heaven
永和宫
Palace of Eternal Harmony
景仁宫
Palace for Scenery and Benevolence
延禧宫
Palace of Prolonged Happiness
斋宫
Palace of Abstinence
奉先殿
Hall for Worshipping Ancestors
奉先门
Gate for Worshipping Ancestors
宁寿宫 Palace of Tranquility and Longevity
皇极殿
Hall of Imperial Supremacy
宁寿门
Gate of Tranquility and Longevity
皇极门
Gate of Imperial Supremacy
九龙壁
Nine-Dragon Screen
体顺堂 Hall of Manifest Compliance
养心殿
Hall of Mental Cultivation
养心门
Gate of Mental Cultivation
寿康宫
Palace of Longevity and Good Health
慈宁宫
Palace of Kindness and Tranquility
军机处 Office of Grand Council of State
乾清门
Gate of Heavenly Purity
九卿房
Ministry for Courtiers
隆宗门
Gate of Great Ancestors
景运门
Gate of Great Fortune
锡庆门
Xiqing Gate
慈宁花园
Garden of Kindness and Tranquility
后右门
Back Right Gate
保和殿
Hall of Preserving Harmony
后左门
Back Left Gate
箭亭
Archery Pavilion
中和殿
Hall of Middle Harmony
中右门
Middle Right Gate
中左门
Middle Left Gate
南三所
Southern Three Halls
右翼门
Right-Wing Gate
太和殿
Hall of Supreme Harmony
左翼门
Left-Wing Gate
弘义阁
Pavilion of Glorifying Righteousness
体仁阁
Pavilion of State Benevolence
文渊阁
Pavilion of Literary Profundity
主敬殿 Hall of Significance and Respect
敬思殿
Hall for Respect and Thinking
浴德堂
Bath Room
武英殿
Hall of Martial Valor
崇楼
Solon Tower
贞度门
Zhendu Gate
太和门
Gate of Supreme Harmony
昭德门
Zhaode Gate
文华殿
Hall of Literary Glory
文华门 Gate of Literary Glory
东华门
East Flowery Gate
西华门
West Flowery Gate
武英门
Gate of Martial Valor
断虹桥
Arch Bridge
内金水桥
Inner Golden Water Bridge
熙和门
Gate of Prosperous Harmony
协和门
Gate of Unified Harmony
午门 Meridian Gate

THE MING AND QING EMPERORS IN THE FORBIDDEN CITY

紫禁城明清二十四帝

MING DYNASTY 明朝 (1368-1644)

Temple Name(庙号): Chengzu(成祖)
Birth Year and Death Year(生卒年): 1360-1424
Period of Reign(在位): 1402-1424
Reign Title(年号): Yongle(永乐)

Temple Name(庙号): Renzong(仁宗)
Birth Year and Death Year(生卒年): 1378-1425
Period of Reign(在位): 1424-1425
Reign Title(年号): Hongxi(洪熙)

Temple Name(庙号): Xuanzong(宣宗)
Birth Year and Death Year(生卒年): 1398-1435
Period of Reign(在位): 1425-1435
Reign Title(年号): Xuande(宣德)

Temple Name(庙号): Yingzong(英宗)
Birth Year and Death Year(生卒年): 1427-1464
Period of Reign(在位): 1435-1449 & 1457-1464
Reign Title(年号): Zhengtong & Tianshun (正统、天顺)

Temple Name(庙号): Daizong(代宗)
Birth Year and Death Year(生卒年): 1428-1457
Period of Reign(在位): 1449-1457
Reign Title(年号): Jingtai (景泰)

Temple Name(庙号): Xianzong(宪宗)
Birth Year and Death Year(生卒年): 1447-1487
Period of Reign(在位): 1464-1487
Reign Title(年号): Chenghua(成化)

Temple Name(庙号): Xiaozong(孝宗)
Birth Year and Death Year(生卒年): 1470-1505
Period of Reign(在位): 1487-1505
Reign Title(年号): Hongzhi(弘治)

Temple Name(庙号): Wuzong(武宗)
Birth Year and Death Year(生卒年): 1491-1521
Period of Reign(在位): 1505-1521
Reign Title(年号): Zhengde(正德)

Temple Name(庙号): Shizong(世宗)
Birth Year and Death Year(生卒年): 1507-1566
Period of Reign(在位): 1521-1566
Reign Title(年号): Jiajing(嘉靖)

Temple Name(庙号): Muzong(穆宗)
Birth Year and Death Year(生卒年): 1537-1572
Period of Reign(在位): 1566-1572
Reign Title(年号): Longqing(隆庆)

Temple Name(庙号): Shenzong(神宗)
Birth Year and Death Year(生卒年): 1563-1620
Period of Reign(在位): 1572-1620
Reign Title(年号): Wanli(万历)

Temple Name(庙号): Guangzong(光宗)
Birth Year and Death Year(生卒年): 1582-1620
Period of Reign(在位): 1620-1620 (one month)
Reign Title(年号): Taichang (泰昌)

Temple Name(庙号): Xizong(熹宗)
Birth Year and Death Year(生卒年): 1605-1627
Period of Reign(在位): 1620-1627
Reign Title(年号): Tianqi(天启)

Temple Name(庙号): Sizong(思宗)
Birth Year and Death Year(生卒年): 1610-1644
Period of Reign(在位): 1627-1644
Reign Title(年号) Chongzhen(崇祯)

QING DYNASTY 清朝 (1644-1911)

Temple Name(庙号): Shizu(世祖)
Birth Year and Death Year(生卒年): 1638-1661
Period of Reign(在位): 1643-1661
Reign Title(年号): Shunzhi(顺治)

Temple Name(庙号): Shengzu(圣祖)
Birth Year and Death Year(生卒年): 1654-1722
Period of Reign(在位): 1661-1722
Reign Title(年号): Kangxi(康熙)

Temple Name(庙号): Shizong(世宗)
Birth Year and Death Year(生卒年): 1678-1735
Period of Reign(在位): 1722-1735
Reign Title(年号): Yongzheng(雍正)

Temple Name(庙号): Gaozong(高宗)
Birth Year and Death Year(生卒年): 1711-1799
Period of Reign(在位): 1735-1796
Reign Title(年号): Qianlong(乾隆)

Temple Name(庙号): Renzong(仁宗)
Birth Year and Death Year(生卒年): 1760-1820
Period of Reign(在位): 1796-1820
Reign Title(年号): Jiaqing(嘉庆)

Temple Name(庙号): Xuanzong(宣宗)
Birth Year and Death Year(生卒年): 1782-1850
Period of Reign(在位): 1820-1850
Reign Title(年号): Daoguang(道光)

Temple Name(庙号): Wenzong(文宗)
Birth Year and Death Year(生卒年): 1831-1861
Period of Reign(在位): 1850-1861
Reign Title(年号): Xianfeng(咸丰)

Temple Name(庙号): Muzong(穆宗)
Birth Year and Death Year(生卒年): 1856-1874
Period of Reign(在位): 1861-1874
Reign Title(年号): Tongzhi(同治)

Temple Name(庙号): Dezong(德宗)
Birth Year and Death Year(生卒年): 1871-1908
Period of Reign(在位): 1875-1908
Reign Title(年号): Guangxu(光绪)

Period of Reign(在位): 1908-1911
Birth Year and Death Year(生卒年): 1906-1967
Reign Title(年号): Xuantong(宣统)

THE FORBIDDEN CITY

紫禁城

本画册为 中 英 法 德 俄 五国文字对照

图书在版编目（CIP）数据

紫禁城：汉、英、法、德、俄 / 旅舜主编. —北京：五洲传播出版社，2009.10

ISBN 978-7-5085-1674-5

Ⅰ. 紫… Ⅱ. 旅… Ⅲ. 故宫—画册 Ⅳ. K928.74-64

中国版本图书馆CIP数据核字（2009）第182257号

※编　　著　旅　舜

※责任编辑　王　莉

※执行编辑　余泯然　赵伟玉

※摄　　影　张肇基　吴健骅　王文波

※封面设计　帅　芸

※版式设计　廖亚平

※本书部分图片由 Getty Images 提供

※Editor in Chief Lu Shun

※Managing Editor Wang Li

※Executive Editor Yu Minran Zhao Weiyu

※Photographers Zhang Zhaoji Wu Jianhua Wang Wenbo

※Cover Designer Shuai Yun

※Computer Layout Liao Yaping

※出　　版　五洲传播出版社

※编　　著　北京精典博雅旅游图书有限公司

※开　　本　787 × 1092 mm　12开

※印　　张　8

※印　　数　1—4000

※版　　次　2009年10月第一版第一次印刷

※书　　号　978-7-5085-1674-5

http://www.旅游图书.cn

Published by China Intercontinental Press

Edited by Beijing Jingdian Boya Traveling Book Co., Ltd

Format: 787 × 1092 mm 1/12

Printed Sheet: 8

Impression: 4,000

Printed Order: First Impression & First Edition in October, 2009

ISBN: 978-7-5085-1674-5

http://www.jdbybook.com

0006000

如发现质量问题，请致电 13371611472 联系调换